Cosmos, God, and Soul

Edward Conklin, Ph.D.

ISBN 978-0-692-26015-9

Acknowledgement

I acknowledge and thank family, friends, and loves. I thank Ms. Natalie Harley for her patience during the task of editing. I also acknowledge and thank my teachers who taught me not to waste my allotted days in the search to know the sublime and numinous depths. Following the prompting of the wise, I searched myself.

Published works by Edward Conklin Ph.D.

A Brief Guide to God and the Soul. (2015). Amazon Kindle and CreateSpace.

In the Beginning: A New Theory of the First Religion. (2014). Amazon Kindle and CreateSpace.

Cosmos, God, and Soul. (2014). Amazon Kindle and CreateSpace.

From Tool-maker to God Maker. (2014). Amazon Kindle and CreateSpace.

Waves Rough and Smooth & the Deep Blue Sea. (2014). Amazon Kindle and CreateSpace.

Getting Back Into the Garden of Eden. (1998). University Press of America.

Contents

Introduction

A book is a conversation between an author and the reader. The author is an explorer and the reader is privy to the journey and the sights along the way. This work discusses theological and cosmological views of reality, and the concepts of cosmos, god, and soul.

Reality is cosmological, yet humans have always felt a need to imaginatively adorn it with various human-like gods. Early humans at some time or another, explored tracts of wilderness, saw a distant horizon from atop a mountain, looked out over an expansive ever-moving ocean, and gazed upon an immense night sky of stars, moon, planets, and comets. These sublime proportions beckoned early humans to fill them with an explanation of where the environment and life came from. Over time developed a theology, the academic study of a single male god. In general, early theology developed in Middle East cultures and from there spread to European culture.

Other early humans, observing the panorama of existence, also pondered in silent thought and even asked aloud, where did the environment and life come from? However, no audible or visual answer was ever received, only silence and the continuing cycles of the environment, life and death. During the passage of time, inquisitive evolving individuals pondered the continuous motion and change of daily clouds and sun across a vast blue sky, and nightly stars and moon changing against a backdrop of an unchanging vast cosmic darkness. Perceptive individuals wondered about where the motion of the environment came from, how does life grow and change, and what happens when life ceases to move at the time of physical death? Cosmology is the study of the cosmos and its dynamic forces, of how it forms and functions. Generally, cosmology developed in the Hindu and Greek cultures.

All things are relative and in ceaseless motion and change. The universe, environment, and life, is a continuation of cosmological force and not the creation of a theological human-like god. The cosmological heritage of the environment and life is harshness, and therefore, humans are harsh either to themselves or to others.

The artistic word portrait of a human-like god is a human conception and the creative crafting of a theological heritage is a way to soothe the harsh edges of life.

In what follows, I argue against the theological view and favor the cosmological view of existence. However, I do favor the view of a soul that can survive death. My orientation, to coin a term, is that of an atheist-dimensionalist. The theological view of human heritage from a human-like god is a persistent cognitive impairment that must be corrected with the observable truth of a cosmological heritage.

Chapter 1

Science without religion is lame, religion without science is blind.
Albert Einstein

Religion

To comment on the above quote by Albert Einstein, it appears that science has the best of it, better to be lame and to limp through existence seeing and discovering, than to totally lose the ability of observant eyesight as has theistic religion. Theistic religion has intentionally gone blind by turning away from the sensate evidence of a cosmological reality, to instead blindly conceive and promote the subjective unreality of a human-like god. The question is, has the human brain/mind ever sensed the presence of a god that placed things into existence, or did the brain/mind place a god into existence? After duly considering the evidence, it is obvious that the latter is the true answer.

Enough evidence exists to assert the claim that evolving human intelligence projects a human-like god to reside distant from humans. In reality, human intelligence only worships its own higher potential by seeing a separate and greater intelligence outside of human knowledge.

Each lives, knows, and daily observes the truth of existence; life is annoying, frustrating, disappointing, harsh, and lethal. Humans consist of innate subconscious forces of sex, hunger, and aggression that often make a mockery, and often ruin the quality of conscious reasoning. Perplexed by these innate predominant subconscious functions, theistic religions see the human condition as flawed and sinful. The body is moved by incessant biological and psychological forces, and assailed on the outside by the forces of the environment and other life forms. Feeble human intelligence responds by directing attention to a conceived greater intelligence outside and beyond personal experience.

Theistic religion is a simple schizophrenic reaction in the true sense of the word, a split feeling, a seeing double, resulting in an imagined outside human-like god. Human intelligence often finds existence intolerable and so splits and imagines an intelligence separate from and much greater than its own. Yet a greater intelligence is only conceived and believed, never sensed and perceived. A god is the result of a self-imposed split in human awareness, thinking and feeling, a deception that theistic humans tell themselves is real, as a way to find assistance and relief from life. A human-like god is a deception but one that a majority of humans obviously feels comforted by and good about. Fervently seeking better comprehension, human intelligence imagined a human-like god, earlier through visual art, followed by the later art of story.

Four stages of human god-making can be discerned beginning in France and Spain during the Upper Paleolithic circa 50,000-10,000 BCE. Early humans used the mineral red ochre to draw images of animals and human female figures on cave walls. The earliest human-like god was female, represented by drawn, painted, and sculpted stone female Venus figures, and pubic triangles. The Paleolithic art was meant to both recognize the female ability to bring forth life, and was also intended as reverence to Mother Earth. Paleolithic humans regarded the earth as female since they observed the bringing forth of plant and animal life from within her womb of soil, dens, and caves.

The second artistic stage of representing a human-like god or goddess began circa 3,500 BCE in Egypt, Greece, India, and China, by sculpting clay, marble, granite, and bronze. The third artistic stage also began circa 3,000 BCE with increasing development of verbal and written language. Early written language in the cultures of Sumeria, Egypt, India, and China was artistically drawn as pictographic images. Gradually the pictographic and hieroglyphic images were made into more abstract symbols of an alphabet by the Phoenician and Greek cultures. Along with stone, bronze, and painted images, words began to be used to artistically create stories of various gods.

The fourth and final stage of god representation, is the use of written words to fashion a greater god image than any mere stone or metal sculpture. European theologians such as St. Augustine and St. Thomas Aquinas, took the written myth of the Middle East tribal god of the Jews, and fashioned the story into a universal god of western culture. The resultant abstract god of theology exceeds any visible image and is today the zenith of human god making. The artistic word portrait is read or listened to, vaguely comprehended, and remembered by each individual receptive to it, especially the young, poor, and under educated.

Evolving human intelligence realized that a better way to represent a human-like god was required. Sculpted and painted visible gods were only works of art made by humans. A more universal god was needed that made the environment, life, and humans. For this purpose a more abstract artistic medium was required, rather than stone or bronze sculptures to portray a god. Using words only, an unseen and unlimited universal god was fashioned with abstract words and ideas in a contrived story. The book could easily be transported and read, thought about, and shared wherever a person might be.

Through history theologians have promoted the artistic word portrait of a human-like god as a way to protect and save humans from the environment, other humans, and individual errors and behaviors. While labor on the project has slackened somewhat in modern times, work on the artistic word portrait of a human-like god continues. No human authority exists with the ability to guarantee protection to humans. Therefore, a human-like god is creatively imagined and artistically crafted with words to assist humans throughout life.

The main conscious intention for the artistic word portrait of a humanlike god, is to assist humans to save themselves from the environment, other harmful living forms, and fellow humans. A human-like god also serves to rescue the individual from the innate lower subconscious biological functions of hunger, sex, and aggression within. Such is the pitiful human situation.

For a connoisseur of religion, the word portrait of a human-like god is read, comprehended, and appreciated as a work of art to contemplate. While for the average person's casual reading and lack of comprehension and knowledge, the word portrait must resemble a stick figure.

Art and Craft

The term art is defined as, "works created by human skill and imagination." Like tool-making, invention, and the creative arts of drama, literature, painting, and sculpture, the many gods and goddesses of religion, are also the result of artistic endeavor. A god or goddess is the artistic expression of creative imagination and talent. Since religion is not a science, it must be rightly and realistically grouped among the arts. Artistically, life is made more aesthetically pleasing by theologians who craft, and by theist converts who promote the artistic word-portrait of a human-like god. The god of religion must be studied for what it really is, a creative and imaginative artistic expression.

Religion is not mathematics and is not objective science, therefore it must logically be a subjective work of art. A human-like god is objectively untrue and false, as each and every god is only subjectively true as a work of visible or verbal art.

Most individuals are too busy with challenges of daily existence, and spend little if any time being creative or artistic. Like many non-artistic individuals who frequent art museums, the majority of the population attend religious rituals and read scriptures and books that present the artistic word-portrait of a human-like god. They read about a human-like god who performed acts of creation, punishment and reward, and who has attributes such as being all-wise, forgiving, just, good, gracious, loving, and merciful.

The word-portrait of a god has long been an appealing artistic work of art to many. Like all good art, the word portrait has been touched up and maintained over the years but has now reached and passed its structural integrity to endure the ravages of time. In modern parlance, as sustenance for the human psyche, its maximum shelf life is expiring.

From a distant past to modern times, the portrait of a human-like god has been artistically crafted with words in scriptures and commentaries. A human-like god is analogically conceived to resemble humans, and is projected from the brain/mind outward and upward. Analogical conception of a human-like god occurs in the early stages of childhood development. Jean Piaget (1896-1980) has shown in his work, *The Child's Conception of the World,* that children model a human-like first father god on parents. The psychological tendency from childhood and into adulthood to think in terms of a first parent creator, was appropriated by theologians and dogmatically crafted over time with words into a human-like god. Scriptural stories about a god form an artistic word portrait to contemplate and to comfort through a life time, and also when the time of life comes to an end.

It is wise of the religions of Judaism and Islam to not let their god be portrayed as visible art or image. If they did so, the visible image would have been too close to all of the other artistically sculpted and painted human-like gods. Only abstract words were deemed suitable for a distant unseen human-like god. Christians eventually strayed by favoring a father figure of a human-like god mentioned as a metaphor by Jesus, and graphically painted on the Sistine Chapel by Michelangelo.

A human-like god is always conceived and never perceived. The human-like god of theology exists only as an abstract word portrait, a substitute lettered symbol and human rendition for a cosmological reality of space and time. The artistic portrait of a human-like god represents limited human comprehension, a human rendering for what is unlimited and beyond, and that moves all things into, through and out of existence. A human-like god is an explanation for the beginning of existence, now time events in terms of reward or punishment, and the future. A human-like god is an invention to explain time, of what began relative inanimate motion and animate behaviors.

A human-like god is offered to the public by theological theme-park like, imagineers, who in imaginative sermons direct attention to the artistic word portrait of a god.

The cognitive act of turning toward and accepting the artistic product of a human-like god, is the act of obtaining an ally during life and death. For many, turning to a word portrait of imagined higher potential is better than turning to the lower potential of a human ally. Only an eternal super ego can affect or change conditions for the better and save the human ego from the often harsh changes of time. A human-like god portrayed in theistic scriptures and writings is a theological artistic depiction, a product offering to individuals who cannot save themselves from a spectrum of harmful and hopeless life experiences.

The unknown origin of the environment and life is humanized by humans, and therefore any human-like god is a subjectively glorified human. Any scriptures of Middle East religion such as the Bible, Quran, and the Book of Mormon, contain no objective truths. Theistic documents are all subjective literary works of art, word-painted testaments of glorified anthropomorphism to explain existence, life, death, and the human condition. Theological religious writings are worthless as they contain no objective truth whatsoever. The theistic documents are valuable only as subjective and aesthetic works of art.

The few religious documents that contain objective truths are the nontheistic Hindu Upanishads, written teachings of yoga, the teachings of Buddha on meditation, and some of the philosophical aphorisms of the Greek philosopher Heraclitus and the verse of the Chinese Tao Te Ching.

The two main genres of literature are fiction and nonfiction. The genre of fiction is further subdivided to include science fiction, romance, poetry, and humor. I propose a new obligatory subcategory of fictional literature to be recognized and established for the future of humankind. The artistic scriptural word-portrait of a god should also be classified as it truly is, theological fiction.

Glamor

The English word glamor came into use during the 1700s and has an origin in the Scottish word, grammar, meaning to learn, and glammar, meaning, the art of casting magic spells or making of charms, meant to allure and to fascinate. The early meaning of the word was to, cast a spell on a person, to influence them to see in a certain way, to make attractive or to make an attraction where none would naturally exist.

Since existence is often deceptive, harmful, and lethal, there has in the past and continues to exist a human need to glamorize existence, to see reality in a less threatening way so as to make life more tolerable. A human-like god is the subjective glamorization of existence. It is the business of a theologian, priest, minister, and theist follower, to glamorize existence for themselves and other individuals. They seek to cast a spell of words and thought and thereby to attract others to join in and accept the verbal and written word portrait of a human-like god.

In a daily reality where trust and love is often difficult to find among fellow humans, just to think there is a human-like god of love who can provide assistance is alluring and fascinating. It is very easy to fall under the subjective spell and to think in this way when taught while young, and even as an immature adult. The magnified glamor of pleasurable ideas of perfect trust, love, and protection, is alluring and is difficult for many to pass by.

Just to think of a human-like god, in an instant, transports the thinker from a painful situation to an imagined pleasure and relief of transcendental assistance and protection. Reveling in the subjective ideational pleasure of a human-like god is a refuge from and a way of eliminating the excess pains and evils of unforgiving daily life.

Alter Ego

In the twentieth-first century, humans continue to grope for an answer to the question of where life came from. Even intelligent alien visitors that pilot UFO's have been added to the marketplace of ideas.

The answer for early evolving humans to the question of where life came from, was that the interior of the earth gave birth to plant, animal, and to cave-dwelling humans. Paleolithic humans first conceived of the earth as a great mother that gave birth to all of life from within her greater form. Just as so many myths suggest, for early historic humans, caves were the place from which life came from on the inside through an opening to the outside, observed to be mimicked in human birth.

Based on research findings, early Paleolithic human groups probably numbered twenty-five to thirty individuals composed of five families. Governing authority was probably and variously by the physically strongest, the best provider, the most intelligent, a shaman with extrasensory abilities, or by coalition of a few. It is probable that during this time that a favored deceased father was glimpsed in subconscious dreams to be recalled on awakening. If experienced by a number of individuals, mutual dreams of a favored male individual may have been passed down by verbal story. In this way the deceased was given special archetypal status as first father. Over time, an archaic first father began to be consciously imagined by those so inclined, and was eventually hypostatized to be a real human-like god.

A god is a human-like governor. There is a tradition by dictators, kings, presidents, and political representatives, to ally themselves with a governing human-like god. Over time political leaders have financially supported the development of theology, the academic study of a human-like god. This was done so for the purpose of governing.

European and Western culture adopted the Middle East biblical fable of a human-like male god that previously inactive, when suddenly, once upon a time, inexplicably became active. Then using only thoughts and words, he made the environment and life. "In the beginning God created the heaven and the earth. And the earth was without form, and void; and darkness upon the face of the deep. And the Spirit of God moved upon the face of the waters. And God said, Let there be light: and there was light." (Genesis 1:1-3)

The biblical Genesis and Garden of Eden story is not based on perception of objective reality but on an artistically inspired story. The story is a feeble and poor attempt to solve an unknown beginning of the environment and life. The story also offers an explanation of how humans came to live a miserable life of toil, hunger, sex and reproduction, and aggression. Having no knowledge about the beginning of a time sequence extending back through generations of parents and grandparents and beyond, there developed a simplistic Jewish theological notion of a first father god. In the Genesis story the fatherly god brought the environment and life into existence by use of mere thoughts and words.

Based not on observable evidence, the biblical analogical reasoning of the god is similar to humans who get an idea to make something, and proceed to speak about it. Generating the view of a human-like first father god, at once provides an explanation of where the environment and life came from. The imagined god also provides an unseen ethical authority to replace a serious lack of ethical and intelligent human authority.

A human-like god is an alter ego of humans. Humans in need temporarily release themselves from their own limited and often ineffectual ego by directing attention to the greater ego of a conceived god. Having a human-like god at least in thought if not in reality, offers protection from the environment and other humans, and relieves but does not completely remove the fear of death. Having a human-like god allows humans to face the unknown, and to remain optimistic despite many and varied struggles and sufferings. The myth of a human-like god is also exploited to gain leadership of a group, and has always been approved of and supported by religious leaders, rulers and politicians. Many humans prefer to be governed by a glorified human-like god rather than by human authority. This preference can be seen to function as both distrust of human authority and as more democratic, as each answers to the god alone before whom all are equal and also before whom all will be judged.

A god is a conceived symbol, a shorthand way to organize human thoughts about an unknown reality of past, present, and future.

The human ego finds it difficult to survive on its own, only the greater ego of a human-like god can give assist an individual to survive through life and an afterlife. Individual life is beset with evils of inside cravings for food, sex, and aggression. Humans also deal with evils outside that humans wreak upon each other, other harmful life forms, and the environment. While some responsible individuals seek personal balance through their own efforts, others seek a human-like god to balance or relieve the evil excesses of life. Finding few helpful humans on earth, necessitated imagining a higher helping presence beyond the earth. Just as there are individual and social benefits to an imagined Santa Claus, and the Easter Bunny, so there are benefits of having a human-like god.

Theologians, ministers, and priests babble on about a human-like god to those who would listen and be convinced. Those converted to theism in turn prattle to others who may join with them in a show of mutual emotional support of the view. Humans gather together to honor a human-like god outside and separate from themselves, yet in reality, they honor the usually unachieved higher potential inside themselves. The mechanism involves use of imagination to conceive a human-like god inside the brain/mind, and then project it to the outside to be shared as a word depicted highest authority of where things come from. The god provides much needed protection and safety on earth and after death. Conceived inside the human brain, the model of a god is projected outside, where all peoples have duly placed their human-like gods in differing times and locations.

Having a human-like god who eternally exists beyond space and time, then humans can prayerfully beseech the god to also continue to exist forever after death. This is just the human ego. Theologians who promote a human-like god are in reality only promoting mere human egoism. The work of theologians is to reinforce the human ego to continue to exist and live. Ego begets ego. Theologians, priests, and ministers exert their individual and collective will to exist and live by projecting the ego of a human-like god to provide outside assistance. Despite struggle and suffering, the individual human will to survive life and death is reinforced by the conceived notion of the stronger will of a god.

Humans gather in a religious group to reconnect with that from which they have come from, to find out how they should live and treat other humans, and to find out what will happen to them after death. The common consensus is that humans come from a rational human-like god who also wants humans to be rational with each other. Conceiving of where things come from as a greater rational intelligence, is also an attempt to make environmental disasters, social conflict, accidents, disease, and death, intelligible and rational.

Eventually shaken in life by experiencing pleasures that eventually through time often become painful, an individual may seek for a way out, to a greater pleasure. For many taught from childhood, the way out is a god. Reasoning reaches its limits to become worn in its efforts to deal with the non-reasoning environment, and just barely reasoning humans. Exasperated human reasoning may then seek a remedy by turning to the imagined greater reasoning of a human-like god. During a theistic religious service, individuals attend to direct attention to a human-like god with the hope that an unseen and abstract word-depicted god, can act for them in life and in an afterlife.

Humans have long observed that life destroys and consumes life. This is the way of existence, and the view human life is special, is bolstered by having a human-like first father god who oversees the processes of both life and death. The concept of a human-like god exists only subjectively inside the human head. The conceived notion that something human-like oversees all things is a confused psychological dynamic of combined human arrogance and ignorance. A human-like god, as the saying goes, can only "help those who help themselves." This is exactly why the concept of a human-like god is generated, to inspire humans with the notion they have help during a difficult life of helping themselves. The existential need for protection generates the theistic concept of a caring father-like god who will help control an uncaring environment, and punish the uncaring evil of fellow humans. This imaginary view of a human-like god is entrenched in the general population. In reality, the theological promise from religious leaders, of help from a human-like god, is seldom kept.

Whenever observing or reading of a person using the word god, it is automatically easy to think how under educated and immature they are. Sadly, most of the population of the earth needs a simplistic explanation of existence. Theistic religion is mainly for children and adults who are cognitively immature and too busy to think and investigate. Everywhere exists the reality of the poor, uneducated, undereducated, the physical and mentally ill, criminals, and violence. Yet sadly, there continues to be an unreal imaginary theistic claim of a perfect and fair human-like god, who observes and presides over the daily assorted madness of life experience.

In religion, the problem of finding out or discovering what or where humans have come from, is an ego problem. The human ego seeks a greater ego for assistance. Individual wanting to survive and prosper generates the human ego, and this personal core concern for oneself that often disregards others, also generates the imagined greater ego of a human-like god. Humans then egocentrically seek to please a first father figure by good deeds and avoiding evil behaviors.

However distant and noninvolved, for many the imagined human-like god remains the preferred way to ameliorate and to escape from the pains of life. The notion of a human-like god represents a greater pleasure to have over the fleeting and often disappointing pleasures of life. A god is the greater pleasure that is the origin of life yet is beyond its fleeting pleasures. Faith is a deluded and misplaced trust in the ideational pleasure of a human-like god, as a way of transcending the changing and brief pleasures and pains of life.

In reality, a human-like god is does not exist objectively, but only exists as a subjective mannequin. A human conceived god is a model with which to drape decorative attributes of the ultra-knowledge of how to make a universe, life, and an afterlife, and is a model of ultra-strength and ultra-protection. A human-like god is an exclusive subjective haven, and does not exist objectively. Yet, theistic religion calls upon individuals to imagine and to act as if there is a human-like god to rely on, for special protection of human life over all other forms of life.

God and Life

Human life experience consists of daily attractions and aversions to people and events. This ambivalence is easily observed in social situations in the tenseness of the body muscles against each other to control or direct mental and behavioral responses. The usual result is cellular and emotional stress, and inner and frequently outer conflict. Subconscious body sensations, emotions, and thoughts affect attention, and flood conscious awareness with ambivalent thoughts and emotions.

Personal peace is always an uneasy truce with circumstances. Humans have to contend with continual change, both inside the body and with the outside environment. Life is replete with many and varied frustrating challenges, choices, disappointments, worries, depressions, and diminished physical ability. Life struggles to endure through stress, injury, illness, and gradual ageing accompanied by mental and physical decline. Each life eventually becomes enfeebled, until youth and health is no more, fled with endless time. Nearing the end of life through ageing, illness, or injury, each individual wishes for a better immediate future. A better future can only be relief from a serious decline of mental and physical life through the peace and oblivion of death. There may also be a hope of leaving the body to enter a dimension of an afterlife.

Life is a construction, an instruction, and a destruction. Life continues until time and death disassemble its parts. Distracted by minute to minute, hourly, and daily short term goals, effectively removes from conscious view the steadily advancing long-term goals of biological life. Subconscious biological life proceeds unerringly to inevitable mental and physical decline, and death. Some few are able to reach an inner poise and peace during life and while nearing death. For most humans, this is near impossible, so why bother? Instead the helpless usually implore a human-like god to remedy the threatening and harmful situations of life and death.

Through long years of evolution, humans have struggled to obtain truths to live by on a little known earth and in a vast mostly unknown universe. Early obtained truths were always pragmatic that also included the grossest of superstitions, including the subjective artistic making of many human-like gods.

Humans have both benefited and have been cognitively blinded and handicapped by their conceived human-like god that exists only within the subject and not as a real object. This is precisely why faith or trust is required. A human-like god is for thinking the best will happen during life and after death. Accepting that a human-like god also exists objectively is optimism, a psychological reaction to counter the pessimistic worst an individual will unavoidably encounter through life.

Participants appealing to a human-like god in a religious service are in reality subjectively appealing to an imaginary model. Though not consciously acknowledged, the real appeal is to a higher level in each other, to act with a higher level of ethics and care, to be at peace and to refrain from harming each other with words and behaviors.

A human-like god is a human fashioned cognitive switch, left off during ordinary events and situations of daily life. Yet the switch is easily turned on again as the need arises for oneself or others. An individual only needs to switch attention from a threatening or harmful situation to a human-like god above it all, and yet incapable of providing life assistance. In times of need, attention switches from subjective individual experience to an imagined objective human-like god as a way of obtaining protection.

Theistic adults teach their children about this pragmatic cognitive switch of a human-like god, and encourage them to turn it on, and turn attention to the subjectively conceived god in times of trouble. In this way, the attentional switch is perpetuated through the generations by instructing the young to turn on their cognitive switch of attention to an imagined human-like god.

Psychological Helper

Humans do not see and cannot fully comprehend the origin of the relative change and motion of the environment and living forms. The underlying motion of this phenomenon is difficult to know. The beginning of relative motion and change is not a phenomenon, it does not appear.

Quantum particles, atoms, electrons, and elements appear but not that which moves these energized particles into existence. The origin of all relative motion does not appear and so is not perceived or seen. To know the unknown origin of motion is why a universal human-like god was conceived and depicted with abstract words.

A human-like god is a psychological helper in the frequently frustrating, frightening, and often futile strain of life experience. Like the image of the helping hand of the food product, Hamburger Helper, the theologically vaunted unseen helping hand of a human-like god fills a hunger need. The imaginary helping hand of a human-like god assuages human hunger for care, and provides humans with the confidence to proceed through an uncaring life stalked by accident, illness, and violence. The helping hand of a human-like god is extended to humans but obviously not to other animals.

As Hamburger Helper provides carbohydrate satisfaction in the stomach and intestinal tract, likewise the helping hand of a human-like god provides psychological and emotional satisfaction. The helping hand of a god also provides safety, and an explanation for the beginning, the enduring, and the ending of life. To say there is no human-like god is life threatening. To have no helper is sensed as disorienting and dangerous, and is to be without support in both life and death. To not have a god is to have no higher authority and standard of right or wrong, good or evil.

Many seek a higher level of personal knowledge. By conceiving, talking about, and attributing better and desired qualities to an imaginary human-like god, humans can imitate and beseech the parent figure for any traits deemed desirable. Humans want wisdom, truth, justice, compassion, and want to be accepted and loved. Humans recognize that certain qualities are good to have, and that only a dismal very few individuals such as saints and mystics are capable of developing them. Desired qualities are then exalted to a higher level and attributed to a human-like god, as a traditional way of being optimistic about existence. Imagining a human-like god with exalted traits is an antidote to pessimism.

Having a role model of a human-like god, the individual can then aspire to emulate and to be obedient, if not to human authority, then at least to a god. In reality, a human-like god does not exist objectively, only and completely subjectively. That there are so many and various gods and goddesses, convincingly shows they are each and all, artistically and word crafted depictions occurring in the human brain.

In an effort to bolster the theistic view, theologians have appropriated and made use of anecdotal stories of another dimensional existence. The stories are of seeing ghosts or spirits, cases of reincarnation, and personal accounts of near-death experience. To these questionable but real experiences, theologians have added an unreal human-like god who dwells in an afterlife dimension, and can assist and comfort the bereaved and the deceased.

Infantile Omnipotence

Sigmund Freud (1856-1939) defined infantile omnipotence, to paraphrase, as a "mental dynamic of an infant associated with primary narcissism, the over-estimation of subjective thought, and an innate developmental inability to objectively comprehend cause and effect reality." The dynamic of infantile omnipotence persists into childhood and is also found in the mental dynamic of adult preliterate societies as superstition and magical thinking. The dynamic is also present in psychological disorders such as narcissism and delusions of grandeur.

Innate in infants, infantile omnipotence is enhanced by having all needs provided by caregivers. Gradually, during childhood, the reality principle of experience reveals a susceptibility to frustration, accident, illness, and pain. The mental dynamic of infantile omnipotence is observed to diminish during childhood, due to the individual observation of himself as vulnerable to situations. The child also gains knowledge that he is not omnipotent due to the consequent and gradual development of realistic cause and effect thinking. Since parents provide comfort, security, and satisfaction of needs, the sense of omnipotence is also projected to parents.

Through maturation, the child comes to realize the parents are also not omnipotent and are vulnerable to harm. The individual is also fueled by the pleasure principle, a lifelong seeking of pleasure and avoiding pain. Therefore, the unconscious dynamic of infantile omnipotence is in adulthood, eventually transferred to a human-like god, having the omnipotent ability to make and care for the environment and life.

The imagined notion of protection by a human-like god is a subconscious continuation of infantile omnipotence. The infant first attributes omnipotence to himself, and eventually projects omnipotence to the parents. Though resolved in adulthood, if instructed in religious views, omnipotence is continued and projected to a conceived and imagined human-like god, a greater omnipotent father figure of caring and protection. The adult view of a human-like god who is omnipotent and who protects only humans and no other living forms, is plainly a case of human narcissism.

A human-like god is also a narcissist over estimation of subjective human thought. Just to have a thought of a god does not mean that the content of the thought exists in reality. Humans have subjective thoughts of unicorns, Santa Claus, and an Easter Bunny but they do not exist objectively, only subjectively. The human prescientific inability to comprehend a reality of cause and effect change, subjectively conceived and crafted the irreality of a human-like god.

Differing Father Figures

The experience of human inability to control cause and effect change, results in the imagining of a human-like god, as a vicarious and ineffectual attempt to influence change. Yet, the greater reality of the vast universe cannot be sanely looked at as the theological effect of a human-like god personality. Children and immature religious adults look at reality in terms of personality and do not think of observing cause and effect change, of how one object changes another. It is cognitive immaturity, laziness to observe and explore, habit, and lack of intelligence, to think in terms of personality beyond what is strictly human.

A human-like fatherly god is said to be the "maker of heaven and earth." (Psalm 146:6) To think of what is beyond human experience as human-like is a human display of pompous egoism. That a human-like god made the environment and rules over existence, it is easy to observe and honest to say, he rules quite poorly.

Christians have a fatherly god who is said to have audibly spoken the words, "Thou art my beloved Son; in thee I am well pleased." (Luke 3:22) The verse states the god loved his son but in another verse the god allowed humans to kill his son for his blood. John 3:16 says "For God so loved the world, that he gave his only begotten son." The god planned and allowed humans to inflict the brutal death of crucifixion of his son, and then received his blood as expiation for human sins.

The god of Christian theology impregnated a young girl and had a son that the god planned aforethought and allowed his death for the original sin of disobedience by Adam and Eve. The god banished the first humans to live separate from himself and his garden, and only by the killing of his son would future humans be reunited with the god and saved from eternal punishment in an afterlife hell. Well, so much for love when humans are asked to love a human-like god that allowed his only son Jesus to suffer and be killed. Christendom (worldwide communities where the Christian religion dominates) is Christen dumb.

The story of Jesus appeals to the poor, uneducated, and undereducated in need of a father figure protector. The story of Jesus is but the human struggle of every person. His life was a transition from the empty rituals of religion and oppressive government, to a cultivation of interpersonal sensitivity, love, compassion, and forgiveness. A supernatural father figure is held out as a comprehensible symbol for cause and effect change and the dimension of an afterlife. The message of Jesus is a way of diverting attention from daily life to a continuing existence in another dimension after the struggle and suffering of life is over.

The life of Jesus has been portrayed to the masses as a miracle that few comprehend and which only faith and belief is required.

Jesus is said to be the begotten son of the god, and all other humans are the descendants of the first humans made by the god. Humans can appeal to the god in prayer as seen in these early (circa 350 CE) verses from the Sinaiticus Codex gospel of Mark.

"Wherefore I say to you, all things whatever you pray for and ask, believe that you receive, and you shall have them. And when you stand praying, forgive if you have any thing against any one, that your Father who is in the heavens may forgive you your offenses. (Mark 11:24-25)

The words of the New Testament contain little beneficial teaching regarding the phenomena of body and brain/mind processes, or observation and emphasis on cause and effect reality. The Christian religion emphasizes a superficial ineffectual mental prayer to a metaphorical father god. The religion teaches no method of individual exploration but instead expects a response from a human-like god. The main teaching of the Christian religion is of struggle and suffering on the cross, death, and an afterlife dimension. The religion also insists on the delusion of a caring father god. These prominent features of the religion bear the stamp of existential irresponsibility, cruelty, and mental impairment. The Christian story has little to do with an intelligent god but rather in reality is only the unintelligent and crazy thinking of humans.

Further impaired Christian thinking is the teaching that salvation is not in the hands of the individual, and that cause and effect cannot be depended upon. Christian theology has pointed out that prayer and good deeds can never save an individual, only an all-powerful imaginary god can save through his grace. Salvation is defined as that "which brings about the preservation of the soul and to escape from destruction or evil." To receive grace, an individual must surrender his life to the total of good and evil he will unavoidably encounter, and hope for the best. Christian theologians have defined grace as an expression of "love and mercy," bestowed not as an earned reward. The act is a desire of the god and is a generosity and a gift of favor and clemency, given by him. Since the god exists only subjectively and not objectively, the cosmological reality of cause and effect change and relative conditions, is the real ruler of each individual life.

The story of Jesus is a lesson in the experience and suffering of life and death. A god cannot suffer but a half-human god can. If a god reproduces himself sexually with a human girl and has a half human son who survives death, then the lesson is that a human can survive death as well. When the human-like god mated with Mary, he became closer to humans and humans became closer to the distant god. Born of a poignant human need to comprehend the origin of existence, a cosmological force was humanized. In reality there is no human-like god and therefore no god's son.

It is eye-opening to contrast the theological father figure of Jesus of Nazareth (circa 6 BCE to 30 CE) with the cosmological father mentioned by the Greek philosopher Heraclitus. (Circa 500's BCE)

"Though the Logos eternally exists, humans have no knowledge of it."

"War is the father and ruler of all; and from it have come gods, and humans, some as slaves and some free."

"It must be known that war is universal and strife right, and that through strife all things come to exist and are useful."

Heraclitus calls a singular transcendental cosmological force that brings forth forms, the Logos. From the Logos comes relative opposing forces and forms that father strife and the conflict of existence. A singular cosmological force divides into numerous opposing environmental and living forms. The originating Logos or cosmological force has metaphorically fathered and brought forth the human-like gods, who are both anthropomorphic causes of and rule the environment. A few of the Greek gods are Poseidon who rules the ocean, and Zeus the sky god of thunderstorms and lightning bolts.

Artistically represented by human-like gods, the awesome powers of the environment oppose feeble human abilities. Humans in turn also oppose each other and by so doing some become free and others slaves.

Humans oppose each other with ideas, personal relationships, sports, the economics of work and business, politics, law, and the military.

Heraclitus contends that war and conflict is the universal condition of existence, and the resulting strife from opposition of forms is an eternal law that is right and just. This is a cosmological breath of fresh air and truth, rather than the stultifying Middle East anthropomorphism of a human-like father.

To conceive of a greater transcendent unseen maker and then to hypostatize it to be human-like and real, and then to further attribute a fatherly caring character to it is quite delusional. The theological fatherly god is a false projection, a reactionary delusion in response to a cosmological reality and the strife and suffering of a brief and often brutal earthly life.

Theism

Humans venture into vast tracts of wilderness, see a great distance from atop a mountain, view the expansive ever-moving ocean, and look up at an immense night sky. For early humans, these sublime proportions beckoned them to fill the vastness with an explanation of where the environment, plants, animals, and human life came from. The human brain imaginatively filled the vast spaces with gods and goddesses.

In some cultures, the view arose of a single tribal god, and this propensity has evolved into monotheism. The theistic cognitive infection of Judaism has spread from the Middle East to Europe, and to the Americas and beyond. The view of one human-like god has been bolstered by the proselytizing religions of both Christianity, and Islam.

A human-like god is said to have passed down to Moses many commandments for the Jews as he referred to them as "stiff neck," rebellious and corrupt. (Deuteronomy 31:26-29) The god thought his stubborn willful people were in dire need of guidance. The theological view of a first father god who's willed commandments should be obeyed, has been utilized to pragmatically form one cohesive social and religious group.

Christians follow only ten of the many commandments of the very same human-like god. The Christian god is in charge of a coming resurrection and afterlife, and functions to dispel the fear of death. The god will also to separate the good from evil into either a heaven or a hell. The religion of Islam worships the same human-like god. Muslims acknowledge a greater will and surrender individual willing to the god five times daily, so as not to forget who is in charge. Are Muslims so forgetful or stubbornly willful that they need to be reminded five times daily in prayer of a greater will than their own?

These three theistic religions have been referred to by academic textbook authors as "great world religions," yet surely this undeserving praise applies only to numbers, and not to any great truthfulness. A human-like god is merely a cognitive tool forged in the human brain and utilized to better survive life and physical death. The theistic god explains the origin of life, oversees how humans should live, and what occurs after death.

A god is an ethical guide. A human-like god is a way of self-limiting human conduct in favor of an authority figure. Following the guiding commands, the individual imposes imitations on himself for the god, and for the benefit of the human group. The human-like god approves of particular rituals and customs. Not to follow them is to risk disapproval by the god, and also risk condemnation by family and the religious group.

Through tradition the view of a human-like god has been fashioned and etched in human awareness. As a child fashions a cutout and uses glue to affix it, the view of a human-like god has been artistically fashioned and then glued to the beginning of existence, to oversee present events, and glued to the ending of life. Yet there is no objective evidence for the existence of a god, the concept has only been subjectively and artistically crafted, and applied to reality events.

Unable to intuitively sense that life is a continuation of the environment, an individual is instead encouraged to focus attention on a conceived ideational projection of a human-like god.

A human-like god is a way of uplifting humans to a higher level of optimism in a difficult life existence. Accepting the view of a god, an individual can communicate with it, be seen by it, and be protected by the god. The viewing of individuals by the god is where authority and ethics is established. Religious leaders and rulers have advocated and made use of the theological ploy of a human-like god as a way of maintaining social order, while elevating themselves above and separate from the general populace.

The average individual spends little or no time pondering or investigating his own puppet-like conditioned life. Instead, many rely on the intervention of a human-like god to improve their lives. Yet the antidote to the struggle of life is to be found in comprehending cause and effect change, not in the subjectively imagined god used to replaces basic comprehension of the environment and life.

A ruling god is always announced by a human who speaks for the god as a prophet. The god given rules are in reality rules derived from the group to benefit the group. Rules said to be derived from a humanlike god serve only to give a better credential to them, so as to increase individual obedience.

There is a danger in having a theological view, as a god will never protect humans from the environment or each other. These days, western culture and governments see themselves as favored by a Christian god's son. In so doing, western culture has been lulled into a false sense of superiority and security.

God Motto

A human-like god functions as a symbol for promoting the group will of a culture. For example, the United States motto of "In God We Trust" placed on currency is a government promoted faith. Use of the motto seeks to promote trust and confidence in governing leaders, and also trust in fellow citizens to mutually accept the money as a legal tender of monetary exchange.

The English word god is generic. There are many gods who have names but the god of the United States has no particular name as do other gods. The English word god is derived from the German word gott, in turn derived from the Nordic gud. The English week day Wednesday comes from the name of the Viking god Wodan, also written as Godin. All of these root words of the English word god, are thought to come from the Sanskrit word hu, meaning, to call upon.

The original motto of the United States is the Latin phrase, E pluribus unum, meaning, out of many one. The motto refers to the forming of a single federal government from the original thirteen colonies and later states. During the Civil War it was suggested that an additional motto, In God we trust, be added to United States currency.

Beginning in 1886 the additional motto was placed on coins. In 1907 Theodore Roosevelt wrote that the phrase should be inscribed on buildings and monuments but not placed on money. In 1956 the United States Congress passed a resolution to add the additional phrase, In God We Trust. President Eisenhower signed the bill into law, and the motto appeared on paper money in 1957 and by 1966 was placed on most all denominations.

Very few countries mention or refer to a god on their money, only Britain, Brazil, and the Netherlands do so today. To recognize the existence of a god on money is to be favored by that god. When a country supports the existence of and has the favor of a human-like god, the god represents the ego of that country and is a symbol of potential domination and exploitation of other countries.

For example, Adolf Hitler's Nazi enlisted men wore a stamped steel belt buckle with the saying, Gott mitt un, meaning, God with us. Interestingly, theistic religion had an influence in the life of young Adolf Hitler who was born 18 April 1889 in the small village of Braunau, Austria. He began public school in 1895, but his religious and devout mother Klara enrolled him in a Christian Benedictine Abbey monastery school for the school year 1897-98.

His mother also seems to have encouraged him to become a Benedictine monk, and he may have entertained the idea for a time. However, he was caught smoking and was expelled. The rest is history.

God and Humans

Gods are conceived in the human brain/mind to control the environment and weather, to protect from disease, and to protect from enemies. Having a human-like god, humans feel relative relief and safer in the environment. After conceiving of a human-like god, and by so doing, having acquired protection for themselves, humans build grand temples and buildings for religious rituals and worship.

The artistic image of a god or his temple is often destroyed during social revolutions and war. The Jewish god Yhwh found it acceptable to visit or to dwell in a small dark room located in the temple at Jerusalem. The room was approximately fifteen feet square and was known as the "holy of holies." The Babylonians destroyed the first temple in 586 BCE, and the god vacated the premises. The human-like god's temple was rebuilt but the second temple was finally destroyed by bellicose Romans.

The human-like god of the Jews did not protect his temple from the Romans who demolished every stone of it. It is recorded by the historian Josephus that after conquering Jerusalem in 63 BCE, the Roman general Pompey profaned the holy place of the god by entering the area where only the high priest was allowed. The Roman general Titus also entered the temple and holy place, before completely demolishing and burning it in the year 70 CE.

Since then, perhaps for safety sake, the human-like god wisely stays far away from his violent offspring. Through the years the god has only been heard from through the spoken words of an occasional prophet or crackpot.

Relief and Safety

The English artist and poet William Blake (1757-1827) said, there are two classes of humans, the "prolific and the devouring" and that "Religion is an endeavor to reconcile the two." The answer to daily frequent human conflict cannot be found on the earth, so the only answer has to be above and out of sight. This is the theistic invisible human-like god of modern western culture.

Relief from the harshness of life and having a safe existence has been and continues for many to be provided for by a reasoning human-like god. In modern times, human comfort and safety is provided not by a god but by human scientific reasoning and the products of its various technologies. However, the relief from life provided by both religion and science lull individuals and cultures into a false sense of security and overconfidence. The reasoning and measuring of science guarantees nothing, and all too often leads to unforeseen problems. The supposed reasoning of a human-like god leads only delusion and often contributes to religious wars.

Despite having the protection of a human-like god, and the best use of human reasoning ability, societies decline, become moribund and cease to exist. This sequence of extinction has occurred for all prehistoric human species. The same has happened to groups of contemporary Homo sapiens, including various North and South American and Caribe Indian tribes, and cultures such as the Sumerians, Hittites, and numerous others.

Human reasoning is often faulty, frustrating, and futile. This is why theistic adherents rely on the greater intelligence and reasoning of a human-like god to rescue them from the pitfalls of life. Theists realize that humans are not capable of living reasonably. Theists prefer to turn away from the worldly folly of attempting to live a reasonable earthly life, and turn instead to the imagined reason of a human-like god.

Life is not safe, so where can an individual find safety in an unsafe world? Through tradition, the average person obtains safety through acceptance of the notion of a human-like god who provides protection during life and death. A human-like god is a mere ideational refuge to turn to in times of trouble.

Theistic religion is the feeble attempt of human reasoning to measure an immeasurable non-reasoning cosmological force. Humans attempt to make existence rational by promoting the view of a human-like rational god, and by relying on the efforts of science. Yet life has its roots in an irrational environment that is a continuation of an irrational non-human-like cosmological force.

Delusion

Life requires minute by minute effort and exertion. The core of existence is evil, an experience of excess stress, struggle, and suffering. This is a fact easy to be reminded of daily by environmental events and hourly news reports

Children eventually grow up to realize that life consists of continuously changing experiences of both reward and punishment. The theological view of a human-like god told to young children and immature adults is a delusion, an imaginative ideational refuge from the continual swinging back and forth though an unreasonable life of hunger for food, aggression, and sex and reproduction.

Annually a number of priests and ministers of every theistic religion meet with an ignoble and illegal end of their sacerdotalist careers as a result of sexual child abuse and sexual affairs with parishioners. The main influence for these sad cases, is not so much personal failing, as it is the unrealistic Catholic rule of celibacy that is based on a delusional view of a human-like model.

The Diagnostic and Statistical Manual of Mental Disorders (DSM-5) published in 2013 is 947 pages in length and contains over 300 diagnoses of mental disorders including seven types of delusional disorders. The view of theism is not mentioned in the Manual but would fit appropriately under the "Unspecified Type" of delusion. A human-like god has been subjectively conceived and is a delusion. A god is a mistaken idea developed to accompany humans through a precarious life journey unavoidably riffled with accidents, illnesses, aggressions, ageing, and to accompany humans on the perilous unknown journey of death.

What is considered good in human life is explained by the model of a human-like god that functions as a raison d'etre, a human reason to exist in a reality sea of environmental and life troubles. With one eye turned to avoid the disapproval of a human-like god, and the second eye turned to avoid disapproval by other humans, each individual struggles through existence. Theistic worshippers raise their faces and hands skyward toward an imagined human-like god of goodness. The subjective desire for a human-like god is a deluded attempt to escape the inevitable personal encounter with evil, the core quality of existence. Life is predominantly evil and only partially good and has never been under the protection of a good human-like god.

Chapter 2

Humans are of two great schools, intelligent scoundrels or religious fools. Al Ma'arri

Father and Son

Humans live in a limitless sequence of time. It is difficult to discern a beginning and ending of the environment and life. A human-like god is generated in human thought and placed at the beginning and ending of life. It was surely observed that children disobey parents and elders. Therefore analogically, in the Genesis story, the first humans are portrayed as disobeying a first father god who banished them to make their own way through life.

Jews use the term father (ha'av) to refer to a personal human-like god who made the first human from the soil of the ground. A story artist from the tribe of Judah, conceived of humans as coming from a first father by being formed "of the dust of the ground." (Genesis 2:7) Not an auspicious origin, perhaps a better material could have been chosen rather than soil or dirt. The use of the word father for a human-like god is used fifteen times in the Old Testament.

Jesus used the word father (abba) sixty-five times in the three synoptic gospels, and one hundred times in the gospel of John. The term was used by Jesus only as a metaphor, a way of identifying and organizing thoughts about the beginning of human existence.

Use of the term father is a way of identifying a beginning of space, time, environment, and living forms. The concept of a human-like god is an easy way to imagine the origin of existence. Thinking of a god as a father is a way of identifying the beginning of earthly fathers, and a way of respecting the line of previous deceased fathers. A first father is a symbol of many fathers, the whole line and series of evolved fathers who lived and died in the distant past, and who brought forth, provided, and protected their progeny to enable them to survive.

The theological story that a human-like god had a son is ludicrous. Yet the claim merits investigation. The earliest written scriptures of Christianity compared with later versions, show evidence of manipulative changes through the years by theologians and editor-scribes.

The Christian religion has from the beginning appealed to the vulgar, (Latin vulgus, common) the average individual of a population. The average person has limited comprehension. For the average person, if something or someone can relieve the emotional fear of death, this would be of great value. A human-like god is an imaginary talisman, to protect humans supernaturally, beyond the natural protection of cause and effect change. The inspiring gospel story of the physical death of Jesus and his body restored to life by a human-like god, is a way of reducing the great fear of mors mortis.

During the years 50-350 CE, the Christian religion grew more rapidly in Rome than in its place of origin in the Middle East. The population of the city of Rome numbered approximately one million. Only fifteen percent were members of the upper classes of patrician and plebeian. The proletariat or working class owned little or no property and were the largest resident group. Rome had a large population of slaves, as many as one-fourth to one-third of the population. The Christian religion grew rapidly among the downtrodden and undereducated proletariat and slave population. This was especially true following legalization of the religion by the Roman emperor Constantine in 313 CE. As the Christian religion grew in numbers, it began to attract influential members of the population. However, the teachings of the religion appealed mostly to the proletariat and to the slave population as is evident in Paul's Epistle to the Galatians in the Roman province of Galatia.

"But when the set time had fully come, God sent his Son, born of a woman, born under the law, to redeem those under the law, that we might receive adoption to sonship. Because you are his sons…So you are no longer a slave, but God's child, and since you are his child, God has made you his heir." (Galatians 4-5, 7, NIV)

The above words attributed to Paul of Tarsus (circa 5-67 CE), are theological pandering and propaganda. The person or persons are told that if they convert to the Christian religion of the human-like god's son Jesus, the hearers will then be accepted as adopted sons of the god. The words are a pitch to join a larger family and to have the protection of the father god and his son. If the hearers convert, they would continue to be slaves or toiling proletariat workers. Yet, they would also be the god's adopted children, and an heir and so inherit what the god has that can reduce the fear of death. Of course this would be an afterlife dimension and a resurrection of the physical body.

The resurrection story is a way to pander to slaves and the proletariat or common people, the "sheeple," as a crude way to reduce the pain of living and the fear of death. Evidence of the intent of Christian editors, scribes, and theological authority to pander and to convince the gullible, can be plainly seen in the earliest extant gospels, written circa 350 CE in the Greek (koine) language. The early gospels are the Sinaiticus, Vaticanicus, and Syriacus Codices.

Scholars agree that Mark is the earliest written of the biblical gospels. In the earliest gospel versions of Mark, Jesus is not portrayed as the son of a god. The first line in the later traditional gospel of Mark is missing that announces, "The beginning of the gospel of Jesus Christ, the son of God" (Mark 1:1) In the early Codex Sinaiticus it simply states "The beginning of the gospel of Jesus Christ." (Mark 1:1)

It is also interesting to note that in the traditional Mark gospel, there is no virgin birth story as mentioned in the Matthew and Luke gospels. The gospel only mentions the baptism of Jesus by John the Baptist, meeting four of his later followers, fasting in the wilderness for forty days, and healing others. There exists no genealogy as in the gospels of Matthew and Luke.

Chapter 16, the last chapter of the earliest Mark gospel contains only eight verses. Later traditional versions contain an additional twelve verses that portray the bodily resurrection and interaction of Jesus with his followers, and a sitting in the presence of a human-like god.

In the early versions of the gospel of Mark, at the end of Chapter 16 it is plainly marked after the eight verses, "The gospel according to Mark." This remark by a scribe in turn overseen by monastic authority, indicates there are no other verses. This is the truth of what happened in the life and death of Jesus. The early Mark gospel is the truth while the later versions of Mark and the other three gospels are blatant theological false elaborated additions. The following are translated verses of the early Codices version of chapter 16 of Mark.

"And when the Sabbath had passed, Mary Magdalene and Mary the mother of James, and Salome bought spices, that they might come and anoint him. And very early on the first of the week they came to the sepulcher, the sun having risen. And they said among themselves: Who shall roll away for us the stone from the door of the sepulcher? And looking up they see that the stone had been rolled away; for it was very great. And they entered the sepulcher and saw a young man, sitting at the right side, clothed in a white robe; and they were amazed. But he says to them: Be not amazed. You seek Jesus the Nazarene who was crucified; he has risen, he is not here: see the place where they laid him. But go, tell his disciples, especially Peter, that he goes before you into Galilee: there you shall see him, as he said to you. And going out they fled from the sepulcher; for trembling and astonishment had seized them; and they said nothing to anyone, for they were afraid." (Mark 16: 1-8) The gospel according to Mark.

From the time of the early written gospels to the later gospels, a scribe and monastic authority, chose to dishonestly elaborate by adding a made-up fictional ending to the gospel of Mark. The glaring dishonest differences between the earliest and later versions of the gospel of Mark, show evidence that the gospels of Christianity were crafted into an emotional appeal with a purpose to exploit the average person. The later additions to the Mark gospel are a false and blatant appeal to relieve the pain of life and to escape from the great fear of death, a possibility that most everyone would be desperate to accept. The verses on the resurrection were added later to the earlier gospels. Those who did so were not the faithful, intent on adding true words to the story.

The verses were added by unscrupulous and deceitful rogues as a way of appealing to the vulgar, a manipulation by the clever of the foolish and fearful unthinking common person.

The resurrection of the body is an appeal to ignorance. In popular thinking of the time, resurrection of the physical body was most important and this is why Christians insisted on burial of the body rather than the Roman practice of cremation. It was thought that the body is the real person, and the false hope developed that the individual would be able to keep the same physical body. The notion of a dynamic soul was not demonstrated or fully accepted to be real, and this is why the insistence on the physical body to be resurrected. Living in later medieval times, the Persian poet Rumi (1207-1273) remarks on the problem of sensing the reality of the soul. "Body is not separate from soul, neither soul from body, yet no man hath ever seen a soul." The concept of a soul was weak or nonexistent while the subjective view of a human-like god was widely accepted.

A human-like god is only a subjective metaphor; therefore, the body will not resurrect. The gospel story of Jesus portrays how he was betrayed by untrustworthy and punitive fellow humans. A human-like father god is held out as a dependable support. The god does allow the individual to die but in a future time will resurrect the person in the very same body. The thinking is, since a human-like god made the first human bodies, then a god could also bring the body back to life. Only the gullible, fearful, and unlearned could possibly accept the view of a human-like god and a resurrection of the same physical body.

The myth of resurrection considers the body as more real than what animates it. The myth of resurrection of the physical body is an earlier false conception that was replaced by an afterlife dimension to which the soul journeyed to after physical death. Adding later additional verses to the early gospel of Mark to show a resurrection and a human-like god, is a way of demonstrating an overcoming of physical death. This could only be accomplished by an all-powerful human-like god.

Son

In the Aramaic language that he spoke, Jesus referred to himself as bar nashi, meaning, a son of man. The phrase refers to human qualities, a son of the human line of descent, a human descendent, a phrase used in place of the personal name. A modern synonym is the phrase, human being. When Jesus spoke of his abba or father, he used it as a metaphor not literally. Jews of the Old Testament used the term fifteen times to refer to their god as a first father, who they thought made humans.

The Hebrew version of the Aramaic phrase bar nashi is, ben adam, meaning a son of Adam. The phrase is used one hundred-seven times in the Old Testament. The term is used ninety-four times by an unknown voice in the book of Ezekiel, not as a term of respect but in a pejorative sense, as a weak and less than satisfactory person.

The Aramaic word bar, means son, while nashi, means a person, having a mortal body fashioned from the earth, weak and vulnerable to the conditions of life and the environment. Since Adam was created and mortal, then Jesus is also a mortal son. He was made a special god's son by scribe theologians as a despicable act of deception toward the gullible and foolish.

As a son of humans or a son of Adam, this is in truth what Jesus exclusively claimed for a total of eighty-one times in the gospels. No one else refers to Jesus by this phrase, neither the disciples nor the writers of the gospels. Since Jesus declared eighty-one times that he was a human son extending back in time to Adam, his words are credible. The phrase, son of man, occurs fourteen times in Mark, thirty in Matthew, twenty-five in Luke, and twelve times in John. Obviously, it is safe to assume that Jesus knew who he was better than any later scribe editors of the gospels, who put words in his mouth to be a son of a god.

The gospel writers put the words "son of god" in the mouth of Jesus only five times. He is referred to as such seven times by other persons, and several times by the narrator of the gospel, for a total of seventeen times.

One Father

The heavenly father that Jesus spoke of is a way to focus attention to a cosmological force. Jesus said, "I and my father are one." (John 10:30) The words are inclusive of everyone and not exclusive to Jesus as theologian scribes have implied by manipulation, omission, and addition to the biblical texts. Jesus is also quoted as saying, "And call no man your father upon the earth: for one is your father, which is in heaven." (Matthew 23:9) Whether an individual can realize his oneness, as Jesus did, is doubtful.

The words referring to Jesus in the modern gospel of Luke 24:51 "and he was carried up into heaven," are not in the earliest Luke gospel of the Sinaiticus Codex written circa 350 CE. Also in the modern version of Luke are over ten thousand added words that are not included in the early Sinaiticus Codex.

Just as every living human is a continuation of and therefore one with their earthly father, so they are a continuation of and one with a cosmological force that has brought forth all things. The father of Jesus is not a theological personality as promoted by sacerdotalist theologians, but a cosmological force. A cosmological force fathers, or brings forth all things into existence, and is immanent in them as an animating force called the soul.

Chapter 3

It is not to be forgotten that what we call rational grounds for our beliefs are often extremely irrational attempts to justify our instincts.
Thomas Huxley

Cosmological

Only recently has human intelligence evolved to the level of being able to comprehend a scientific reality. Yet from earliest times humans have attempted to comprehend when, how, and from what the environment and life came to exist. Even in modern times, the demands and duties of life, such as work and relationships, leave precious little time to ponder important questions and arrive at satisfactory answers. Most humans have to be satisfied with daily use of pragmatic conceptions and ideas.

What could possibly be the impetus for the motion of the universe, environment, and living forms? What invisible force forms the concatenation of elements of energy, shapes galaxies, stars and planets, and on earth forms amino acids and the proteins of life? Whatever exists as a cause of change cannot be spied with the pulp of a three pound brain that constructs the limitations of space and time, and imposes a causal sequence on changing events.

In awe and fearful of a continually changing universe, environment, and life, humans sought for a way to influence the processes of existence. For early humans, the cause of the constantly changing environment and life, was imagined to be a human-like god.

The antecedent of relative existence is not a human-like god ancestor but a cosmological force that moves and drives all into, through and out of existence. A cosmic force that drives all things into existence by parting into relative time as energy particles that combine to form the environment, which life on earth is dependent upon. The same cosmological force also drives all things out of existence via change, ageing, and departing death.

Early people observed thunder and lightning storms to be discrete, has a boundary or edges, and a beginning and ending time sequence as it moved over the land. Through the cognitive process of animism, humans perceived the storm as exhibiting a human-like willing intention. In this sense, early humans were correct, the movement and behavior of life has a continuity with the motion of the environment. The reality of what moves the changing environment outside, that same reality of change exists inside of cells and organs of the body.

Drive

The biological-psychological term, drive, is defined as "biological behavior brought about by deprivation from what is necessary for life." Hunger, sex, and aggression are defined as drives. Living forms are seldom at peace, they are moved and driven to survive by hunger for food, sex and reproduction, and aggression.

In environmental temperate zones during the spring months of the year, the driving forces of life in vegetation are palpably sensed by animal and human alike, as a freshness and quickening of energy. New growth of plant life consists of the driving forces of life revived from the dormancy of winter. Vegetation seeks for nutrient food in the soil below, grows to sexually reproduce through roots or seeds, and aggressively competes for growing space and sunlight.

Evident in all life forms including reasoning humans, life is ever driven by subconscious non-reasoning forces of hunger for food, sex and reproduction, and aggression. These drives are only partially under the control of human conscious reason. Moved and driven by subconscious unreasonable primary biological forces, secondary conscious reason can only struggle, can only guide and direct the primal unreasoning relative forces that function to preserve the human body. Humans are driven through existence by unreasonable forces that unerringly drive an individual to satisfaction but also to many troubles.

Relationships are satisfying but also lead to conflict. Hunger for food drives an individual to satisfaction of the appetite, and also contributes to the troubles of diet, nutrition, and health.

Sex and reproduction drive an individual to seek love and to have children. This dynamic also leads to divorce, custody battles, and heartaches. Aggression drives an individual to compete and to survive but also leads to the troubles of conflict and violent death.

The legal system struggles with social problems and crime by insisting on the criteria of what a reasonable person should do in a particular situation. The legal trial system also insists on the criteria of innocence or guilt beyond a reasonable doubt. But reason is only the evolved conscious surface of the brain cortex, while the midbrain and body are the real determinant and subconscious driving forces of behaviors.

Early Concepts

The Greek concept of moira, or fate, is based on the perception of being moved and driven through life by a non-personal and greater unknown mover and weaver of relative events. The Greek derived word irony, is the sense of limitation of human awareness of the causal process, so much so that what is expected differs from what eventually occurs. Therefore a situation is ironic. The Roman view of fatum or fate is derived from the Greek moira view of existence.

The Hindu and Buddhist concept of karma is the law of cause and effect, the view that a change in one thing drives change in another as a related time sequence. This view is also that of modern science, and the theory of hard determinism. Hindu thinkers theorized that life was a link in a chain of cause and effect supported by the environment, and intuited that the environment came into existence from a greater cosmological force they called Brahman.

The human-like god of Judaism, Christianity, and Islam, is said to predestine human lives, meaning the god foreordains every event through eternity. In Islam predestination by the god Allah is called kismet. Through providential foreknowledge, the god predestines which humans will be saved and which will be damned. Yet the omnipotence and omniscience of the human-like god also leads to the philosophical problem of evil.

If a god has willed the beginning of existence, then the god must will the present progression of life with all of its strain, stress, suffering, and evils, and also wills the eventual physical death of each individual.

The three attributes of the western human-like god are said to be omniscient or all-knowing, omnipotent or all-powerful, and omnipresent or everywhere present. A nonhuman-like cosmological force can only be said to be omnipotent as it moves all things into, through and out of existence, and omnipresent as all existing nonliving and living forms are equally and immanently a continuation of it. A cosmological force is not omniscient, it is blind and unknowing as it functions to drive all related things into relative motion. Each human stands surrounded by continual and unrelenting motion and change. Life, the earth, sun, stars, galaxies, and all that exists, is a continuation of a cosmological ocean of changing motion.

Cosmological Aryan View

Circa 500's BCE in northern India, an Aryan Hindu by the name of Siddhartha Gautama became known as the Buddha or Awakened One. He claimed to have reached insight into what he called sankhara, meaning, willing, and tanha, craving. The individual has to reduce both to a minimal willing calm of nirvana so as to bring to an end the endless life cycles of reincarnation. Siddhartha Gautama, was mythically said to have reached enlightenment on a full moon night in May. This is an obvious symbol of full inner and outer illumination. Buddha awoke to that which moves and drives the individual through endless space and time, as relative karma of cause and effect. The man Buddha whom many continue to hold in the highest regard, reached the zenith of insight and comprehension of life and existence. This was accomplished without the assistance of a human-like god, and without measured experiment of science.

The feat of enlightened comprehension was accomplished through intuitive sensing of how body function and individual willing is identical with and is a continuation of a cosmological force. There occurred a perfect seeing resulting in a perfect ethic. While difficult if not impossible for the vast majority to experience, the Buddha continues to serve as a beacon of inspiration for the few with interest and dedication to explore.

Theological Aryan View

Circa 1200 BCE in the country known today as Iran, an Aryan by the name of Zoroaster, founded the religion of Zoroastrianism. Unlike his Aryan descendent Buddha, Zoroaster took a less insightful view of existence and anthropomorphized a single cosmological force into theological human-like twin god figures of Ahura Mazada, the good deity of light and truth, and Ahriman, the evil deity of darkness and lies. A follower of the religion then had the personal choice to will good thoughts, words, and deeds, or evil thoughts, words and deeds. Individual choices resulted in the afterlife destination of a judgment, and either a heaven or hell. According to historians, this way of thinking has been shown to be the influence and basis for the later theological views of Judaism, Christianity, and Islam.

Semi-Scientific Methods

Archaeological evidence shows that the practice of yoga originated in the Indus Valley area of ancient India as early as circa 3200 BCE. In an attempt to better comprehend both a cosmological origin and human life, through the centuries the Hindu culture developed semi-scientific disciplines of yoga dating from circa 700 BCE. Those who experientially developed and practiced various yoga disciplines observed and passed on the observations as verbal and text teachings, such as *Patanjali's Yoga Sutras*. Hindu writings mention the personal benefits for those who practice the mental-physical and ethical disciplines of yoga. Results were observed and empirically commented on but there was a lack of testing.

The practice of Buddhist meditation dates from circa 530 BCE and is also a semi-scientific discipline. Through meditation practice based on verbal and written text instruction, Buddhists calm and focus attention with the intention to experience meditative insights and ethical sensitivities.

Results were observed on the benefits of those who practiced meditation, and the non-benefits of those who did not practice meditation. Yet, like the discipline of yoga, while results were experientially and empirically noted and communicated, there was a lack of testing.

Non-Scientific Religion

The Christian religion began in northern Israel circa 30 CE. The religion grew in numbers predominantly in Rome by circa 300 CE. The Christian religion began as a Jewish sect and eventually spread beyond the Middle East and Rome to other countries in Europe. In the Christian religion, there was no emphasis on at least semi-scientific observation and no verbal or written texts on practice. Having no prescribed discipline of observation and practice, emphasis was on following the stories of the miraculous feats of a human-like god and a supposed son of the god. Both were said to be located in a spiritual dimension from which either might assist the individual on earth, or might save or punish in an afterlife.

In European cultures there was no emphasis on observation and measuring until after the Bubonic Plague that began in Italy in 1348, and spread to other countries. The plague killed at least one-third of the population of Western Europe. This event occurred in spite of prayers and pleas to a human-like god and his son who never intervened. The grip of the stultifying cognitive infection of the Christian religion that entered Rome, Italy circa 50 CE, was later loosened by the abrupt arrival of another swift and much more virulently convincing biological infection that also ironically began in Italy circa 1348 CE.

The cognitive infection of Christian theism and the biological bacterial infection of Yersinia pestis met head on. The bacterial infection quickly won out over the long term and even more insidious cognitive infection that a human-like god and his begotten son cared about and protected humans. The lowly bacteria accomplished what no single human or group could do, it cleared away the conceptual cobwebs of European theological thinking.

One cannot help but wonder if a similar plague would be a therapeutic remedy for the Islamic religion, and the theological terrorist turmoil in modern times.

The biological bacterial infection of the Bubonic Plague cleared away a cognitive theistic infection. For the first time in Europe, observation, measuring, and thinking about the environment began to be practiced and to flourish during the late Renaissance in the 1500's. Copernicus, and later Galileo, Leonardo Da Vinci, and other Humanists of the time advanced the acquisition of knowledge. Out of the freedom of non-theistic observation and measuring, the scientific and empirical method of experiment, slowly and surely developed.

Order and Disorder

Modern humans began to evolve circa 150,000 years ago, and slowly learned to conceive the origin of the environment and life to be made by human-like gods. This was a way of imposing order on many random reality events. Early religious rituals of killing and offering of the blood of life to a humanlike god was intended as a plea for intervention to insure order and prevent disorder.

Early humans surely wondered how the sequence and order of the environment and life came to exist, and had to have wondered even more about how disorder came into existence. In theistic religion, a human-like god is given credit for the order of existence, and either humans or an evil devil, is usually given credit for the disorder.

Human narcissism conceived a human-like god that made the Garden of Eden environment. In the mythical Genesis story, an ever-existent human-like god created the orderly paradise and made the orderly life therein. Shortly after this event, came sin or separation from the god, and the disorder of existence caused by the rudimentary intelligence of the first humans. As punishment, the god banished and sent humans out of his small-ordered paradise of Eden, into the much greater disorder on the earth he had also created.

To this day and hour the god continues to allow disorder on earth, and only at a unknown time will the god impose future order by resurrecting humans, and then by separating the orderly humans from the disorderly into a heaven and a hell. Through centuries, European and Western cultures have accepted this Middle East mythos.

Rationality

Discounting the religious myth of a human-like god, other humans evolved to intelligently reduce the disorder of existence by developing culture, government, and science. Life is predominantly irrational as evidenced by the attempts of many cultures to rationalize it by conceiving of so many human-like gods.

Human history is a long evolutionary process of trial and error learning. In recent times, the close observation and measuring of science developed to investigate the order and disorder of the environment and life. Modern science has successfully discovered and comprehended order, and is able to predict events of disorder, such as weather, earthquakes, and disease. In discovering cause and effect order, science also encounters just as much disorder such as destructive climate cycles, explosive supernovas, comet and asteroid impacts, that destroy both terrain and life.

Contrary to theistic religious myth of a once perfect order, life is both an orderly and a disorderly experience, evolving from both the disorder and order of the environment. The environment evolved from the disorder and order of energies and relative forces, all imposed by a singular cosmological force. From a singular cosmic force came simultaneously both order and disorder. As the prophet Zoroaster announced thirty-two hundred years ago, both order and disorder are eternal twins.

"In the beginning there were two primal spirits, twins spontaneously active, these are the Good and the Evil...." (Yasna 30:3) The twin spirits are Ahura Mazada of truth and light and Ahriman of lies and darkness.

From a singular primary cosmological force, secondary relative forces and forms of the environment and life are borne through cause and effect change of relative order. Once relative order exists, disorder then intrudes as chance and opposition. Life proceeds through the disorder of competition, conflict, disease, ageing, pain, and death. With the order of relative forms, comes the reality and necessity of disorder.

Early Views of Order and Disorder

Archeological evidence from India dating to circa 3200 BCE, shows an early Hindu method directed to reduce disorder and promote order of the human body and brain/mind through the discipline of yoga postures and meditation. The physical and mental benefits of the ancient disciplines of yoga to reduce stress disorders, continue to be recognized and practiced today.

Circa 530 BCE, a Hindu sage perceived the disorder of existence and life as dukkha, meaning ill-fit-together and suffering. The heroic forest-dwelling ascetic Siddhartha Gautama, later became the Buddha or awakened one. To reach awakening, Buddha used ascetic practices to reduce and subdue the inner disorder producing biological and psychological subconscious forces, of straining for food, sex, and aggression. His was a true focus and effort to reach a high level of personal order. Siddhartha Gautama through effort and trial and error, learned to not overly strain for or to overly strain against, which results in physical and mental disorders. Instead he reached a balance and this became his well-known philosophy of an orderly Middle Way path through life.

The early Greek culture observed both the order and disorder of the environment and life. For the Greeks, what contributed to the disorder of existence was conflict among the various gods and goddesses as found in the religious myths of the culture. The presence of moira (Greek, portion, what is allotted in life) as the fate of unexpected events, also limited individual experience in life. Moira also led to both order and to disorder as portrayed so well in Greek tragedy plays.

The Jewish culture saw disorder as coming from human disobedience, as sin and separation from the order created by a human-like god. In the often dream-like sequence of life events, struggling to live, the Jewish remedy for the disorderly experiences of life was to abstract attention from an immediate reality, by imagining mythic stories of a human-like god of order. Having a human-like god fortifies humans in an effort to attain order and to reduce the disorders of life. To not have a god is to not have enough fortitude to endure the disorders of living.

The Middle East human-like god was adopted by Europe and later by the West to serve as a model of ethics. Human ethics is born from the disorders of communal life, and the right and wrong of getting along with others. Existence is not supported by a human-like god but by a cosmological force. Behind the forms of environment and life are relative forces and energies. Behind all phenomena there is a single cosmological force that produces and supports them. Relative time has been borrowed from the timeless and must return. Assurance about life and death, order and disorder, is sought by humans from a human-like god. Yet little assurance of order on the earth exists, where only insurance is available, which has to be paid for.

Human-Like God

Lacking an earthly good to guide them, humans en masse agree on the psychological maneuver to manufacture a greater good of a human-like god. A god is a way of identifying where the environment and life came from. A god also protects humans from the evils of the environment including accident, illness, fellow humans, ageing, and physical death. A human-like god exists exclusively in human subjective thinking as a feeble light to dispel the gloom of daily stress, struggle, and suffering of life.

The view of a human-like god is an invention inside the human brain, and then vented outside. A human-like god is an imaginary controller of earthly events. The stimulus for imagining a human-like god is born out of fear of the unknown, the environment, fellow humans, and fear of disease, ageing, dying, and death.

A human-like god is a cognitive attempt to be safe and is where care and love can be obtained.

In contrast to the untrue theological genesis story, the true cosmological genesis is the following. There is a timeless cosmological force, transcendent and immanent, that moves all into, through and out of time. It has three immanent and commanding laws for human life.

Thou shall hunger for food.
Thou shall have sex, reproduce, and toil to care for the results.
Thou shall be aggressive in competition, possessiveness, jealously, hunting, killing, and war.
Amen!

The phrase, Mother Nature, is a conceived anthropomorphism for the known earth, just as a human-like god is conceived for an unperceived and unknown cosmological force. On each side of now, is an infinite time of past and future as motion and change. That which moves all that exists of the environment and life, is an omnipresent and omnipotent cosmological force.

Cosmological sin, (Hebrew hata, separation) occurs as the cognitive act of anthropomorphism, the conceiving of a human-like god that the majority of humankind prefers and accepts. Instead of the conceived theological doctrine of, original sin and separation, the replacement doctrine of the twenty-first century is the evidence of continuation and non-separation from a cosmological force.

Chapter 4

*All things are in everlasting motion, out of the infinite come
particles, moving above and below in endless dance. Titus Lucretius.*

Cosmic Force

Everything in the universe is bursting, bursting forth from a
cosmological force into relative parts. Cosmologists call the bursting
forth of existence a Big Bang. Big Burst is a better term. Things
don't bang into existence, they burst into existence and life. From a
cosmological force relative forces of gravity and electromagnetism
and energy of elements have burst forth. Environmental forms of
stars, planets, moons and asteroids, and on the planet earth some
nine million species of living forms, have all burst forth into
existence. Whatever bursts forth as inanimate particles of energy
goes, and what bursts forth as living forms, grows.

A cosmological force bursts forth verb and noun parts of reality
existence. As a continuation of a cosmic force, there is a bursting
forth into the relative motion of elements and environmental forms,
from which burst forth growing and living forms. Both environment
and life exist for some time, age, and then slowly or quickly burst
asunder to go out of existence. Having reached an ending all forms
revert to a beginning. The origin of life is a continuation of non-life,
the environment, energy elements, relative forces, all of which are a
continuation of a cosmological force.

A cosmological force moves all the universes that ever were, is, and
will be. In so doing it does not drop a single thing from existence. At
the basic quantum level of reality, the graininess all energy particles
recede to blend with a smooth oneness, a singularity that exists as a
cosmic ground connecting every relative particle.

By conceiving of a human-like god, religion attempts to describe the
point of contact with a cosmological force. Theistic religion attempts
to comprehend cosmological force by positing a human-like god at
an arbitrary beginning and ending.

The continuation of cosmological force as relative motion inside of human cells and organ function of the body, is called a soul.

Cosmological force is impersonal, and can be only be obliquely known by inference. All relative forces, particles of energy, stars, suns, planets and moons, and living forms, are a continuation of motion relative to a cosmological force. The favorite direction of cosmic force is circles. A cosmological force subtracts to form particles of energy that form concentric circles of subatomic quanta, atoms, electrons, that form the concentric circles of sun, planet and moon orbits, and the immense concentric circles of galaxies. Connected and linked to the concentric motion of energy and the concentric motion of the earth environment are the concentric motion and circular shape of living cells. A cosmological force informs and in a sense tells, all relative and living forms to go in circles and cycles.

What exists has come from an all-pervading and non-human-like cosmological force. As to how or why an impersonal cosmic force exists, began relative motion, and supports all things, is to attempt to answer a question that is metaphysical or beyond the physical. Human ability to sense and to perceive reality is limited. There is no history and no human religious story of a cosmological force, as it is an impersonal surround existent beyond space, time, causality, and so beyond human knowledge. Logic and measures of mathematics are ineffectual in detecting it. Comprehension of it can be obtained by observation and intuitive perception.

Irrational Cosmological Force

The sensory evidence is that inanimate nature and living forms are in motion, not from a human-like god but as a continuation of a cosmological force. A cosmological force is irrational as it cannot be rationally measured or compared with any known thing. A cosmological force is made measurable and made rational only by comparing it to humans as a human-like god. Humans as a species are at best only borderline rational.

This is evident in the continuing irrational theological view of a human-like god that continues to reject the truth of a cosmological reality. From a human perspective, a cosmological force as the origin of existence is irrational. A cosmic force brings forth both good and evil, it brings the environment and life into existence, and yet eventually destroys them through accident, illness, or ageing time. A cosmic force is irrational as it:

1. Does not exist in contrast as shades of color or shape.
2. Cannot be detected and measured and therefore cannot be comprehended or compared with anything.
3. Moves nonliving and living forms into existence and then destroys them.

Cosmological force is immeasurable and is irrational, and so are continuations of it as the irrational forces of life, as hunger, sex, and aggression. It is often difficult to use reason to direct hunger to a good result, as the irrational force of hunger often leads to the not so good result of failing to achieve the rational good of a balanced diet and health. Instead there is often an imbalance of under-eating, over-eating and obesity, and eating of harmful foods loaded with fat, sugars, salt, and additives. It is difficult to use reason to direct the irrational force of sex to a good result. The irrational force of sex often leads to the not good result of obsession, unwanted pregnancy, sexually transmitted diseases, harmful affairs, and domestic violence. It is often difficult to use reason to direct the irrational force of aggression to a good result. The irrational force of aggression often leads to the result of possessiveness, jealously, envy, resentment, conflict, injury, hatred, crime, murder, and war.

The primary relative forces of life always assert their rule to impair human reasoning. Civilizations fragment and decline over time as a result of over-population, disease, conflict, and war. Even twenty-first century humans will not be able to successfully extricate themselves from this inevitable historic cycle.

Since humans find it difficult to reason with irrational forces within themselves and within others, this is why a greater reason is projected to the outside as a human-like god who can reason for humans.

A god is a human cognitive tool to advance from lower to higher levels of rational thinking.

An individual who is persuaded to accept the theological view of a human-like god, wants to advance from a lower to a higher level of knowledge, and wants answers to existential life situations. An individual wants to receive assistance from a god in advancing from a lower to a higher level of economic prosperity, wants safety, and wants to advance from losing to winning aggression in conflicts and wars.

Semi-Metaphysical

A non-physical cosmological force moves physical forms into, through and out of existence. From a metaphysical force a transition occurs to a subtle physical, or semi-metaphysical, known as relative force and energy. Semi-metaphysical is the reality that exists between the metaphysical and physical inanimate and animate forms. Prior to modern detection of forces as gravity and electromagnetism, omnipresent energy of quantum and subatomic particles, and atoms and electrons, there were earlier ways to identify these semi-metaphysical forces and energies.

In Hinduism, Brahman (Sanskrit brh to move, grow) is a word meaning, the ultimate not human-like, not detected by the senses, metaphysical ground of all phenomenal existence. From Brahman came the relative effects of semi-metaphysical energies and physical forms. For example, in Hinduism, shakti (Sanskrit shak, force or power) has long been a word meaning a primordial force or energy that brings forth the changing cosmos. It is conceived to be a female creatress of life. Another Hindu word, prana, (Sanskrit pra, into or enter) means a vital energy present in the breath, air, light, and is said to be concentrated in the semen of males and vaginal wetness of females.

The Chinese word, chi or qi, early referred to steam rising from cooked rice or the condensation of breath exhaled on a cold day. The word refers to the subtle animating energy present in the environment and living things. The term is also used in Chinese medicine and martial arts.

In early Greece, the Ionian philosopher Leucippus (circa 400s BCE) was the first to develop the theory of semi-metaphysical atoms. The theory was based on the view that if an individual took a piece of wood and kept cutting it into finer and finer pieces then one would arrive at the basic parts that made up the wood. Leucippus and his student Democritus called the basic parts, atoms, meaning unable to be cut. The modern theory of energy and elements takes this namesake.

From what has the subtle semi-metaphysical forces and energies come from? This is a problem in modern times. The human physical eye and brain has learned to detect and measure relative semi-metaphysical forces of magnetism and gravity, and the elements of atoms and subatomic quantum particles. Yet a metaphysical cosmological force cannot be detected and measured. What exists beyond the semi-metaphysical and physical is a truly metaphysical cosmological force.

Primitives of the past and the religious-minded of today, conceive of the metaphysical origin of existence to be a human-like god. Modern science today has done better. Based on the evidence of the effect of galaxies moving apart from each other in space, cosmologists advocate a cosmic explosion or Big Bang as the metaphysical cause of all relative motion. In reality, the Big Bang explosion has to be recognized as an effect and not a cause. Only a metaphysical cosmological force can truly be a cause of this phenomenon and other relative effects.

The modern science of physics is concerned with the reality of locating and measuring both mass physical objects, and detecting the semi-metaphysical forces of magnetism, gravity, dark matter, and dark energy. Dark matter and dark energy have no detectable and measurable mass and so have not been observed, only inferred by observing their influence on behaviors of physical stars and galaxies. Dark matter and dark energy may be semi-metaphysical or there is a chance they are the metaphysical origin of all existence. The only truly metaphysical reality is a cosmological force that moves all semi-metaphysical forces into existence.

Dark Matter

There will never be a truer statement in the personal quest for wisdom. The goal of life is to realize how human life is related to the motion of the universe. The quest is to intuitively comprehend how the smallest quantum particles to the largest galaxy and universe, are a continuation of a cosmological force.

Of course no human was present at the causal beginning of the universe, so science is limited to studying visible effects and only speculating and theorizing on a cause, of what changed to become relative effects. The mission of science is to theorize about reality and to observe and measure relative reality processes. Science has not found a cosmological force of which the environment and living forms are a continuation of, that is, not until recently, and not completely. Recently science has found what may be an actual cosmological causal force, or the closest effects to it, and has bestowed the various names of dark matter and dark energy to it.

Astronomers, cosmologists, and astrophysicists, have only recently found that visible galaxies, stars and moons, planets, comets, asteroids make up only about four percent of the universe. The universe is estimated to contain one-hundred billion galaxies, each containing billions of stars, clouds of gas, dust, innumerable planets and moons, and the cosmic debris of asteroids, comets, and meteors. Stars emit energy as radio waves and X-rays that move through the universe at the speed of light. Yet, everything observed is like the very tip of a cosmic iceberg, and ocean icebergs typically are only ten percent visible on the surface of the water. Both calculation and observation confirm the vast universe consists of primal invisible forces that do not emit electromagnetic radiation. These cosmic forces are referred to by science as dark matter and dark energy. A recent estimate is that the universe consists of, twenty-three percent dark matter and seventy-three percent dark energy.

Dark matter was a term first used in 1933 when astronomical observation and calculation of gravitational effects showed that there had to be more matter present in the universe than telescopes could detect. Today dark matter is calculated to make up about twenty-three percent of the universe but can only be detected and observed as a gravitational effect that holds galaxies together. If there were only the gravity of visible matter, galaxies would not have had enough matter to form. They would also fly apart as they don't have enough matter to produce a sufficient gravitational force to maintain their galactic structure.

The total weight of dark matter has been calculated to be six times that of all visible matter. Dark matter cannot be seen as it does not emit light and does not consist of atoms or elements, yet it exerts gravitational force. Astronomers and astrophysicists can observe and measure how dark matter gravitation affects the circular rotation of galaxies and how dark matter gravitation bends the light of objects near it.

Calculations have shown that a huge circular ring of dark matter surrounds the Milky Way and a vast dark circular ring thought to be dark matter has been observed through telescope to be surrounding nearby galaxies. Only the effects of dark matter are measurable. What dark matter is, science cannot measure.

Dark Energy

In 1998, the mission of two research teams was to measure the deceleration of the universe said to have occurred since the Big Bang fourteen billion years ago. However, researchers were surprised and shocked to find the expansion of the universe is not slowing but is accelerating. The unknown anti-gravitational force accelerating the expansion began to be referred to as, dark energy. Various theories of dark energy also refer to it as quintessence, meaning a pure or perfect essence (a term used by the early Greeks for ether, thought to be a fifth element of existence). Dark energy is also referred to as phantom energy, meaning an apparition, an appearance or optical illusion, without material substance. Dark energy has been equated with Einstein's cosmological constant, an anti-gravity vacuum force thought to keep gravity from collapsing the universe.

Use of the word "dark" in the term dark energy, denotes human ignorance of where this force comes from, and just what it is. Dark energy is uniformly distributed throughout the universe and its effect is not lessened as the universe continues to expand. The rate of expansion and acceleration of the universe is measured through observations utilizing Hubble's law. These measurements have confirmed the existence of dark energy, and calculations give an estimate of the percentage of how much unseen dark energy exists.

Today it looks more and more like unseen dark energy is the moving force of the visible universe. Dark energy does not emit or reflect light, has little weight, and does not consist of particles or atoms. As to what dark energy is, only its effects can be observed. Dark energy is not a particle energy, it is a pure force. Since dark energy is not atom or particle matter energy, it is a misnomer and a better term would be "dark force."

This dark force moves not only particles but galaxies through the visible universe. Science has difficulty in accepting the existence of something that is not measurable. Despite the idea diarrhea of measurements and concepts generated by the human brain/mind of cosmologists, astronomers, and astrophysicists, dark energy will remain an immeasurable cosmological force.

Dark energy may well be the cosmic origin of existence. Since dark energy has a uniform distribution through space and time, can it reasonably be said to have come from some other force? Therefore it may well be the true cosmological force. It has been calculated that one hundred billion cubic kilometers of space (about the volume of the earth) of dark energy, would weigh a thousandth of a gram. Its density remains the same in every cubic centimeter of space and does not increase in density in any area. Dark energy is an all-pervading motion, and is expanding the whole universe. Since dark energy is uniformly distributed through space, it deserves the attribute of being omnipresent. Since dark energy moves galaxies through the universe it also deserves the attribute of omnipotence. Not capable of knowing, dark energy can be said to at least know how to move all things into and through the known and unknown universe.

Dark energy is not particle energy but is a primal unseen force that may or may not come from something else. The universe may not be in motion from the explosive concussion of a Big Bang but may be propelled into existence by dark energy.

Some cosmologists speculate and theorize that dark energy could be an effect from another dimension, and only observed in the dimension that humans inhabit.

The effort to comprehend what dark energy is, is said to be the biggest challenge in astronomy and physics today. So much so that in 2008 NASA and the U.S. Department of Energy (DOE) signed an agreement to implement the Joint Dark Energy Mission (JDEM). The cooperative mission will measure the expansion rate and structure of the universe, and will also develop the first space observatory designed to better comprehend dark energy.

Out at the limit of human comprehension is an unseen cosmological force that moves a whole visible universe. Dark energy is uniform, is one form evenly present in space, and does not seem to be destructible. If by chance dark energy has an origin, then it must be related to another primal cosmological force. Relying on human logic, there has to exist a cosmological ground from which come all secondary relative forces and energies. A non-generated cosmological force must generate all things.

Energy is a relative phenomenon and is therefore not a primal cause of the motion of the universe. Only a cosmic force can endlessly bring forth relative forces, energy elements, material forms, and can animate, grow, and re-grow living forms. Each living body is a continuation of a force that moves the universe. There is constant change of the environment of air, clouds, water, soil and tectonic plates of the earth as it rotates on an axis. The earth revolves around the sun that rotates and revolves through the Milky Way galaxy, and moves through a vast little known universe.

A single unseen formless force is without size and time, boundless, moving all from the outside, and as an immanent movement inside. That which moves all into existence is unknowing and uncaring, yet humans can be comforted by knowing that what moves life to form is indestructible, and also exists as an immanent presence within.

The average individual is much too busy with economic survival, idle talk, electronic media, and shopping, to give much notice and be amazed by function of movement occurring within the body.

Nourishment, liquids, air, and temperature move in and out of body cells and circulate through organs. The animating movement and function of life in humans is often called the soul. When movement is referred to in the environment, it is called energy. Both the soul of life and the energy of the environment share one common origin, a cosmological force.

Cosmic Inheritance

The heritage of human existence is not written in any religious text. The heritage of life is written only in the behavior of the cosmos, and in the behavior of environmental forms that are primary to humans. Human life is a continuation of an indestructible cosmic force. Biological function has a cosmological metaphysical basis. The comprehension of this is difficult, and sadly most are not capable of this feat of comprehension.

The movement inside of life, is a continuation of the motion from an outside environment. However, a separation occurs by not perceiving a continuation from the environment, and by not intuitively perceiving the environment has come from a cosmological force. Instead, an inept way of identifying the cause of life is accomplished by conceiving of a human-like god.

Human life is animated by a metaphysical force from which it has come, of which there is little knowledge. Animated life is like a puppet that moves by being pushed and pulled by an unseen force located both outside and inside. Theistic thought says that there is a human-like god puppeteer that is accountable for human existence. The god made and activated the puppet and also pulls the strings of human actions through situations of intervention, reward, or punishment.

Based on methodical observation, science more accurately says existence and behaviors are caused by relative parents and ancestors, nourishment, a supportive environment, by detectable atom and quantum energy, and relative forces such as gravity and electromagnetism. Of these two views of religion and science, the latter is more truthful so far as relative reality can be observed.

Yet, science is limited in its observations of space, time, and causality. Science accurately sees life causally connected, but with little ability for comprehension of a metaphysical cosmological force.

Religion insists there is an animating presence within humans that differs from material and physical form, which is said to be non-destructible, and is called a soul. However, there is no observational evidence for this view. Theistic religion is also handicapped with anthropomorphism, the view there is a human-like god. What can be observed and what requires no blind faith is subconscious and conscious growth within humans, animals, and plants, and the changing motion of the environment and greater universe. Whatever moves through space and time is a continuation of a transcendent field or ground of a cosmological force.

Instinct

Modern psychology has developed the theory of instincts. The word instinct is derived from Latin instinctus, meaning, "arouse, inspire, incite, impel, prick, or goad." An instinct is defined as, "an inherited tendency of an organism to make behavioral responses to environmental stimuli without reason or training."

An instinct is a behavioral response below the conscious level of the cerebral cortex of the brain. Instinctual behavior may occur at a particular stage of development, such as the instinctive nursing reflex shortly after birth, instinctive display of frustration and aggression during early childhood, and instinctive sexual interest and exploration prior to or at the time of puberty. In animals and humans, instincts make up the will to exist and to live and compels the individuals of a species to survive.

Behavior is instinctive if it occurs without prior individual experience or learning. For example, baby sea turtles after hatching from their egg instinctually head to the ocean. Various bird species build nests that they have never observed being built. Butterflies migrate two thousand miles or more for the winter and summer seasons to a location they have never seen.

Sigmund Freud (1856-1939) argued for the existence of instincts. Sex is a life instinct he called Eros while aggression is a death instinct or Thanatos. Other researchers such as Abraham Maslow (1908-1970) have argued that for humans, sex, hunger, and aggression cannot be considered instinct as they can be consciously overridden. Maslow's view that humans have no instincts can be seen as an attempt to rationally exclude the non-rational functions of instincts. To say there is no instinct in humans is plain wrong, and is only a rational attempt to do away with what is not rational.

For humans it is instinctual to acquire and ingest food, to seek a partner and to have sex, and to be aggressive, all primary to reason. Early structures of the brain began with vertebrate evolution circa 500 million years ago. Evidence suggests that what is referred to as the reptilian brainstem, the mammalian brain, and neo-cortex of the brain, co-developed as three differing structures situated on top of, and connected to one another. Each of the three brain areas are interconnected as one holistic brain, but retain their own unique kinds of intelligence, such as memory, movement, subjective sense of self, and other vital functions.

The brain structures originated in rudimentary form with the early vertebrates and evolved in size and function during the process of evolution. The three cerebral layers also appear during development of the human embryo and fetus, and in so doing repeat the long chronological evolution of animal species growing in size and function, from early vertebrates and reptiles to modern humans.

The oldest and most primitive structure of the human brain is the R-complex or reptilian brain, located beneath, and to the back of the forebrain and comprises the brain stem. The reptilian brain is shared by all vertebrate animals evolving 500 million years ago beginning with fish, and has remained almost unchanged through the long process of evolution.

The primitive reptilian brain functions for self-preservation as instinctual behaviors of aggression, territoriality, and to dominate for both food and sexual reproduction.

The reptilian brain also functions to stimulate the reflex behavior of ritual displays as a nonviolent way to dispute for mates, territory, and food, through gesture instead of violent conflict ending in death.

From reptiles evolved early mammals. The word, mammal, is from the Latin word, mamma. The word refers to the biological trait of mammals and the motherly breastfeeding of milk to the young. It is generally theorized that early mammals began to evolve from reptiles about 285 million years ago. Many of these early species became extinct circa 245 million years ago, but some survived to become ancestors of mammals such as birds and a weasel-like rodent. Remains of the small weasel have been discovered in at least six geographic locations and dated to about 200 million years ago.

The mammalian brain which is the mid-brain of humans is also known as the limbic system, a circular area surrounding the brain stem and composed of areas including the hypothalamus, hippocampus, amygdala, and others. Affective functions evolved in the mid-brain such as playful moods, moods associated with reproductive behavior, parental behavior such as female nursing, feeding and protecting the young, a sense of identity, and memory. These evolved mammalian structures and traits of the brain are also present in birds and some fishes, and so suggest an origin with early vertebrates.

In humans, instinctual sexual behavior is regulated by the hypothalamus, located in the mid-brain directly above the pituitary gland. The hypothalamus stimulates the pituitary through neural connections and hormone-like substances that stimulate sexual behavior via hormones of the endocrine system. The hypothalamus also regulates appetite and hunger. Some have observed that having a satisfying sexual relationship helps to control overeating. By satisfying one area of the hypothalamus, the area for appetite and food is also satisfied.

Sex and hunger are not the only functions of the body controlled by the hypothalamus. In addition to sexual satisfaction, it also controls and regulates growth, heart rate, metabolism, aggression, thirst, breathing, digestion, sweating, wakefulness, body temperature, and fear responses.

Through the autonomic nervous system, the hypothalamus maintains homeostasis of heartbeat, breathing, emotional arousal, and many other vital functions.

In rudimentary form, the neo-cortex (new brain) evolved in the early vertebrates and continued to evolve through the primates and reached its most developed form in the human species. In humans, conscious thought and reason evolved including conceptual abilities for language, writing, reading, mathematics, and logic.

Midbrain

The human midbrain exerts a primary instinctual influence over cerebral brain functions. Anyone who has attempted to lose weight or to fast from eating and has consciously sought to deny the instinctual need for food, knows firsthand the strength of the instinct for nourishment taking place in the midbrain that can override all reasoning from the cerebral cortex. Anyone who has consciously sought to deny the instinctual need for sex or attempted to be celibate knows firsthand the strength of the instinct that occurs in the midbrain that can override all reasoning. Anyone who has attempted to control anger and aggression and has sought to deny or prevent the instinctual need to express it, knows firsthand the strength of the instinct for anger and aggression as a midbrain function that can override reasoning.

The amygdala consists of two almond shape structures of the midbrain. Research has shown they perform a primary function in processing of memory and emotional reactive behaviors of fear and aggression, and also desire, pleasure, and nurture behaviors. Studies show conclusively that when Caucasians are shown photographs of dark skin Africans, the amygdala are activated in a fear response. The darker the skin, the higher the amygdala fear response.

Another observed phenomenon of response to the color black is, Black Dog Syndrome, or black dog bias, observed and anecdotally reported by veterinarians and animal rescue and shelter workers. The term refers to the incidence in which black dogs and black cats are passed over for adoption, take longer to be adopted, and are euthanized in greater numbers than are lighter-colored animals.

No scientific research has been conducted on the phenomenon. Speculation on causes range from a fear of larger breed of dogs such as Rottweilers and Dobermans, or the conjecture that it may be a carry-over effect from the superstition of bad luck associated with black cats.

The fear response to the color black as a precursor to aggression or avoidance is instinctual and subconscious. All efforts of idealistic reasoning by legislators, judges, and the legal system that seek to legislate and enforce laws of racial equality are doomed. A number of studies show the subconscious functions of the amygdala override all conscious reasoned preference and idealistic conceptions of equality by the cerebral cortex.

The will to live and survive, is located throughout the cells of the body, and in centers located in the cells of the instinctual midbrain. It is these centers that coordinate and impel behaviors of hunger and eating of food, sex and reproduction, and aggression.

The cerebral cortex of reasoning and conscience is often shocked while witnessing some of the more extremes of midbrain behaviors such as over or under eating of food, harmful sexual practices, and the senseless aggression of violent crimes and wars. The cerebral cortex wants to comprehend, influence, and rule, but the ability of the cerebral cortex to form images of memory and imagination and to reason and measure, is no match for subconscious influence of the will to live of the midbrain functions. The will to exist and live is composed of three powerful forces of hunger for food, sex and reproduction, and aggression. The cerebral cortex does not rule but only seeks to regulate these instinctual subconscious forces and behaviors with custom, religion, and law.

Life Force

The will to live as hunger, sex, and aggression immanent in the individual and the species, is a continuation of a cosmological force. The origin of existence is an unmeasurable force both transcendent and immanent as cause and effect change, and the will to live is a continuation of it.

Individual life is the endeavor to explore and balance a cosmological immanence expressed as the will to live, as hunger for food, sex and reproduction, and aggression. These three forces are a continuation of a pervading cosmological force that moves all existence.

From differing relative forms has come opposition, the origin of aggression and destruction, and for life is the forerunner of the aggressive eating of other life forms and their death. From the very beginning of time of particles and forms, an affinity and attraction has existed and is the origin of life and sex.

In order of sequential human development, following the sexual act, conception occurs followed by an embryo stage, and then the fetus. As the fetus develops, hunger and obtaining nourishment enable survival of the new life. Following birth and during infancy and childhood, during interaction with others, aggression develops. At the time of puberty, sex and the ability for reproduction develop. Each of these three forces make up the core of the will to live, and is essential for survival.

Sex and reproduction insures the continuity of species and families, while forces of hunger and aggression function to preserve individual life. Sex and reproduction of life mimics and is a continuation of a cosmological force that brings both nonlife and life into existence. The aggression of life mimics and is a continuation of a cosmological force that naturally destroys galaxies, stars, suns, and planets.

Cause and Effect

The English word cause is derived from the Latin word, cauda, meaning tail. The word effect is derived from the prefix letter, "e," to mean out, and the Latin word, facere, meaning a making or doing. The word cause denotes what moves, sets things in motion, and changes things as an animating sequence of effects. Human awareness is limited to personal space and limited in time as past, present, and future, and usually has an impaired comprehension of causal sequence.

Humankind has recently developed the methodical method of science to recognize the regularity of change as effects and trace them to the change of a cause. Where there is relative change there is a causal force, and what propels compels. For the environment and life to exist there has to be a compelling force from which both have evolved.

The efforts of science rests in the method of observing and measuring changing phenomena, and also by seeking laws of regulative change. Science offers no absolute, only the relative regularity of change that rules all with beginning and ending, and determinism of cause and effect.

The semi-orderly struggle and carnage of life is evidence of a single unintelligent cosmological force. Not a theological intelligent god but an unintelligent cosmological force has evolved animal and human intelligence. An ever untiring cosmological force pushes out relative forces, energy elements, and environmental forms into the space of where it exists. That which pushes out never tires while all of what is pushed into existence eventually tires. For living forms quiescence exists in bacteria and plant forms, and animals and humans retire as the need of sleep overtakes the individual. Eventually humans retire from the work and struggle of living to rest in old age, and eventually retire from existence by dying and death.

On a subconscious level, humans comprehend that all things in this earthly dimension constantly change in time, comprehend how illusory things are, and comprehend the vanity and the eventual worthlessness of all things. Many humans turn away from this conscious awareness to look for a way to tolerate existence and to be optimistic about it. Humans accomplish this by conceiving of a human-like god who by having a greater intelligence will assist and be supportive of them. Yet there is no evidence of an intelligence moving the universe. There is only evidence of relative forces and energy elements.

Chapter 5

Like walking across a sharp blade edge, the way to the soul is narrow and difficult, say the wise. Katha Upanishad

Thoughts on the Soul

Science is a continuing progression of observing and measuring whatever it can, as it seeks to comprehend causal relationships of relative forces, energies, and forms. But this is its limit of observation and induction. Science has not found a soul or mind within human function; only a brain and biology of cells, organs, and behaviors. All parts of cells and organs are named, categorized, measured, dissected, diagramed, and functions explained.

Science explains that life is a function of energy. Science, to its credit, has observed and amassed much evidence for the function and change of environmental, geological, and biological evolution. Biological evolution is explained as an interaction of environment and living organisms.

The dynamic of human behavior, both inside and outside the body, is explained by the science of psychology known as Operant Conditioning or Behaviorism, developed by B. F. Skinner (1904-1990) and others. The psychology states that a human body is only biological within, and consists of behaviors that are conditioned by the environment. Animals and humans consist of stimulus and response behaviors. Behaviorism is a physical and biochemical explanation of life, and therefore excludes any metaphysical view of function and behavior.

Human dynamic of brain and body function is better revealed, yet still inadequately, by Sigmund Freud and his schema of Id, Superego, and Ego structure. Dynamic functions of the mind are discussed, such as unconscious and conscious complexes, psycho-sexual stages, projection, and repression. Yet these functions continue to be grounded or have a basis only in physical and biochemical processes, and therefore lack a metaphysical basis.

Looking within at the content of conscious awareness, is observed a twofold function of willing and knowing. Of this twofold function, knowing is traditionally over emphasized as the most important and as the metaphysical function in humans. Yet the evolved ability of knowing is secondary to subconscious biological cell function which is primary.

Knowing consists of inner brain images of outer sense objects in now moments. Images of the past appear as memory, and images of the future appear as imagination. Intuitive perceptions appear as do conceptions of reasoning. What else appears in conscious awareness?

The word usually used is volition, or more properly, willing. In conscious awareness there mainly occurs willing of hunger for food, for sex and reproduction, and willing of aggression. Conscious willing awareness is supported by subconscious willing of cells to exist and function, the willing function of organs, and willing of muscles to move. Humans think of themselves as the physical body, and usually not as the energies of cells and organ function.

Living forms have both a metaphysical origin and a physical function of form. Therefore they should be classified as, semi-metaphysical. Many humans confuse themselves by seeing their body as the result of being made by or as coming from a human-like god, rather than as a continuation of forces, energies, and the supportive environment.

Many think of their soul as conscious thinking ability of reasoning, judging and ideas. However, three forces of the body, hunger for food, sex and reproduction, and aggression, function to preserve life and to survive. These same three powerful forces and functions are prime candidates for what is referred to as the human soul.

Freud and the Non-Metaphysical

Sigmund Freud (1856-1939) was of Jewish heritage, was an atheist who did not accept the view of a human-like god, and he accepted reality to be only physical.

He was not receptive to notions or experiences of what is said to be metaphysical. In his book, *Civilization and Its Discontents*, Freud mentions what a friend of his referred to in a letter as an "oceanic feeling," a sense of eternity and a spiritual feeling of being unlimited. Freud goes on to comment that he does not think the oceanic feeling is associated with any metaphysical reality. He wrote the experience is a remnant of the newborn's ego that originally was not differentiated from the world, and only slowly did the child's developing ego gradually narrow to form a sense of self or ego separate from objective reality.

For Freud there was no human-like god, and no unseen soul inside of humans, only unseen biological instincts residing in the unconscious Id. The Id was Freud's psychological terminus and he searched no further into the mystery of the relative origin of life. Atheistic and scientific, there was no metaphysical importance of the instinctual forces of hunger, sex and reproduction, and aggression. Freud said that the instincts originate from "somatic organization" but he did not discuss what organizes the cells of the body from which the instincts originate.

Writing in his work, *New Introductory Lectures on Psychoanalysis*, Freud states, "We approach the Id with analogies: we call it a chaos, a cauldron full of seething excitations….It is filled with energy reaching it from the instincts…." He thought that the Id strives to bring about satisfaction of the instincts. In philosophy, analogies are classified as fallacies of relevance, are conceptual and not perceptual, and therefore not correct. Freud's use of analogies clouded his and other's clear comprehension of the metaphysical origin of the instinctual forces of hunger for food, sex and reproduction, and aggression.

Modern psychology has investigated what researchers refer to as instinctual and innate drives of hunger for food, sex and reproduction, and aggression. Researchers such as Robert Ardrey, (1908-1980) Konrad Lorenz, (1903-1989) and Erich Fromm, (1900-1980) and others, also see instinctual functions as innate and exclusively biological.

However distant, biological function is related to and draws impetus from the environment that, is in turn related to and draws impetus from transcendental energies and forces as revealed by quantum theory.

At this juncture, an important distinction has to be made. Instincts are both biological and psychological forces. Hunger, sex, and aggression, are felt as forces in the subconscious cells of the body and cerebral brain cells of conscious attention. The felt forces of obtaining food, sex, or aggression, both direct and distract conscious attention. Both functions appropriately fill conscious awareness and forcefully direct attention, so that effort can be expended to correct a specific deficit or excess, or to obtain a particular goal.

The individual forces of hunger for food, sex and reproduction, and aggression, are often difficult to deny. The task of everyday life is to moderate these three powerful forces. An individual cannot overly antagonize or conquer these strong subconscious and conscious forces. An individual can only respectfully make peace and seek to better direct them.

By becoming more familiar with the strong instinctual force within, it is possible to intuitively trace these individual forces to a single metaphysical force. Subconscious instinctual forces of life root in and grow from the environment that in turn is rooted in a single cosmological force; therefore life exists and endures.

Glamorous Soul

Spending excess time alone, an individual finds they become painfully bored, they then seek to be with others for relief. In a very short time there may arise boredom with others. The individual may then seek a change of company, or solitude once again. Comfort is fleeting and easily changes to discomfort. Since life consists of discomfort, pain, and suffering, existence is glamorized by conceiving of a human-like god. Existence is glamorized by having a god, and human life is glamorized and made special by having a soul that survives death.

Theistic religion says that the human soul is judged by a human-like god, and has either a conscious existence after death in either a heaven or hell, or an unconscious existence until a bodily resurrection.

Hindu seers also glamorized a transcendent soul or atma, residing inside the human body. When realized through meditation and ascetic practices, the atma is described as consisting of an essence of freedom and bliss. This suggests that when the non-blissful distractions and stress of mental and bodily experience are subdued by ascetic practices and yoga, only then is the blissful atma revealed.

This is an error of attribution. Buddha more accurately perceived not a transcendent blissful presence inside but a "house-builder," that built or constructed the body. The perceiving of the body as containing a transcendental presence is true but it is not blissful at all; on the contrary, the soul is the main contributing cause of human struggle and suffering.

In reality, the Hindu bliss experience occurs only when freedom from the atma or soul is achieved. Bliss attributed to a transcendent atma is a false attribute. Bliss comes only from transcending the subconscious soul forces of hunger, sex, and aggression, to perceive them to be a continuation of a cosmological force. That which moves the individual physical body to exist and to live are the forces of hunger, sex, and aggression. The conscious transcending of these subconscious forces is the origin of bliss. The individual freedom attained is from the soul force that drives life. Achieving this, no human-like god appears to welcome the liberated individual, only personal awareness of a transcendence of existence.

Psyche Symbol

Psi is the 23rd letter of the Greek alphabet. It forms the prefix of Greek words such as psukhe meaning breath, and psykhe or psyche, meaning soul. The prefix psy, forms the English words psychology, psychiatry, and psychic. The word psychology literally means, soul knowledge. Yet, modern psychology has become more interested in studying the mental or mind functions of the conscious and subconscious brain, and also behavior.

Many psychological studies and theories exist regarding memory, imagination, attention, perception, and conceptual processes. Little research has been conducted as to whether the soul exists or what the soul may actually be. Closely examined, the early Greek view is informative as to what the psyche or soul consists. Symbolically, the early Greeks were on the right track of the psyche or soul as evidenced by the shape of the psi symbol that suggests that the soul is triune, it is composed of three parts diverging from a beginning point extending into existence. The Greek letter psi Ψ can be seen to be an intuitive perception of a beginning from the depth of a bottom point to extend into the upper stem of the letter. This can be seen as a beginning and extension from one cosmological force and trifurcating into three relative soul forces. The upper center is the extension of sex and reproduction as a direct continuation of a cosmological force, while the two sides of the figure can be seen to be the twin forces of hunger for food and aggression.

Psyche

Circa 700 BCE, the Greek poet Hesiod wrote a poetic work entitled, *The Theogeny*, meaning, birth of the gods. In the work, the arche or beginning of the cosmos was chaos, meaning not disorder but a primal infinite space. In this vast primal space there came into existence Gaia the earth, and then Tartarus the depth of space beneath the earth that also contained the afterlife of Hades. The fourth to exist was the human-like god Eros, who is associated with and represents the primal force of life, sex, and reproduction, and who later on in the story married Psyche or soul.

There are many stories about Psyche but essentially she was once a beautiful mortal woman who men and gods turned to adore and to court her. Aphrodite the goddess of love and beauty, became jealous of Psyche and ordered the god Eros to cause her to fall in love with the ugliest man to be found. Instead, Eros fell in love with Psyche and took her to his secret abode. Eros hid his identity and warned Psyche never to look on his face but one night when Eros lay sleeping, Psyche glimpsed his face. Awakening, Eros left not to return and Psyche in despair searched for him.

The looking of Psyche upon the features of the god Eros, and then the god leaving to be separate from Psyche, may represent how the soul is separate from, longs for, and seeks to be in the company of a primal cosmological force as represented by the figure Eros. A further meaning is, that evolved human reason is poignantly unaware of and lacks transcendental apperception of how it is a continuation of a cosmological force.

In a later myth, Aphrodite made Psyche to perform four labors which she accomplished successfully, and she was then reunited with Eros. Zeus transformed Psyche into a goddess and she married Eros. The story characters reveal a profound truth, that the human soul is considered to be mortal and separate from its origin. Yet, in reality the soul is immortal, and sex is an intimate bond with and continuation of a cosmological force.

In Greek and Roman art, Psyche is portrayed as a human-like goddess with butterfly wings. The art and story suggests how the soul as symbolized by the butterfly image, and marriage of Psyche and Eros, is a continuation of a cosmological force. The force of sex and reproduction is connected to the beginning of the cosmos and anthropomorphized as Eros, the "fairest among the deathless gods, who unnerves the limbs and overcomes the mind and wise counsels of all gods and all men." The god Eros is a continuation of a cosmological force that only appears as Chaos, a primal space, from which all things come from and are contained in.

Eros was later and variously depicted as a youth or young man with wings, sometimes portrayed as bearing a gift for his lovers such as a rabbit, chicken, or goat. He carried a bow and golden arrows, or torches to inflame sexual desire, and could often be indiscriminate by inciting a person to incest, homosexuality, and bestiality. Once released from his bow and penetrating the target, his arrows of love were not easily extracted or removed and afflicted both humans and gods

The strong force of sex and reproduction is the main essence of the human psyche or soul. This metaphorical Greek view is much more clear and sane than the deluded view of sex in the Middle East.

The Greek metaphorical and philosophical insight is that the individual psyche or soul consists of the primal force of sex and reproduction that in turn is a continuation of primal cosmological force. This view is light years ahead of the doltish Jewish view of the Garden of Eden punishment of acquiring the good and evil knowledge of sex, of the view of Sheol and having no soul that survived, and the views in the book of Leviticus that sex was polluting. Compared to the Greek metaphorical insights of the soul, these Jewish views are ignorant and deluded.

The Christian view of sex is also ignorant and deluded. According to Paul of Tarsus, sex is a "thorn" of the flesh. (2 Corinthians 12:7-10) St. Augustine spoke of sexual concupiscence as original sin that separated humans from a theological conceived human-like god. Christians banished sex to a biological function of the body and the earth that brought only suffering of life and death. In Christianity, sex became a devil, the force of opposition, conflict, and suffering to survive life, and the toil of husband and wife to support children. The sexual force of the flesh that Christians crazily see as of the Devil, is but one of three relative expressions including hunger for food and aggression that are the animating triune soul, as a continuation of a sole cosmological force.

A cosmological primal force as Chaos, and Eros as sex and reproduction, evolved the psyche or soul to be immortal and to survive physical death. From a primal cosmic force evolved sex and reproduction and the related individual soul or psyche of living things including microorganisms, vegetation, animals, and semi-rational humans.

For humans at least, the psyche survived physical death. For early Greeks, the last breath of a human psyche was thought to transform into a butterfly, a visible image of an invisible coherent force that survived physical death. The early Greeks considered butterflies to be the souls of the dead. In some early Greek paintings there is an image of a small winged stick figure that resembles a butterfly, and represents the psyche or soul leaving the head of the portrayed deceased person. The human-like god Eros and his wife psyche are sometime depicted with butterflies around them. Like a butterfly or "flutterbye," the soul or psyche also journeyed.

The Greek view of the time was that the psyche journeyed to the afterlife of Hades. Pythagoras, Orpheus, and Plato also advocated the view of metempsychosis, to move beyond death as a psyche in another living body. The Greek mathematician and philosopher Pythagoras (circa 570-495 BCE) taught the view of metempsychosis, of recurring lives as both animal and human. In the teachings of Orpheus the psyche or soul was born, lived in a physical body, and died but the psyche went through a grief-filled cycle of metempsychosis or palingenesia of many lives. Only through practice of ascetic discipline and initiation rituals in which secrets were revealed, could the individual eventually reach oneness with the gods, especially with Dionysus the god of sexuality. In Thrace during the 300's BCE there lived a religious group of ascetics known as Ctistae, probably associated with Orphism, who practiced celibacy and who acted as philosophers and seers.

The Greek philosopher Plato (circa 424-348) writing in his work *The Republic*, tells the story of a soldier by the name of Er who was killed in battle and came back to life after twelve days. Upon reviving just prior to being cremated, Er told his story of how as a psyche or soul he travelled to a place of judgment where some souls were directed to go under the earth and some to the sky. Some also chose future lives as animals or humans.

Plato

The Greek philosopher Socrates (circa 469–399 BCE) relied on reason and the Socratic method of comprehension, as a way of enquiry into philosophical interests. This was accomplished by arranging a series of questions and answers or dialectics, to eliminate contradictions of reasoning as an exercise to reach a balance of agreement deemed as a search for the good.

Plato (circa 424–347 BCE) a student of Socrates, conceived of the psyche or soul as consisting of three parts and functions. The most important and main function of the soul was reason, the ability to think and to seek knowledge and wisdom. Another function is the spirited or the emotional, the need to be approved of and be accepted, including anger and aggression.

The third function of the psyche was appetitive, the desires for food, drink, sex, and money.

The nonphysical soul could be polluted by an excess of spirited emotions and appetitive desires that clouded reason, so that at the time of death and separation from the body, it was drawn again to an earthly life. Plato taught that the psyche or soul survived physical death and returned to live again in a cycle of metempsychosis or reincarnation. Plato reasoned that as the opposites of heat and cold exist, there must be an opposite of the change of physical death. This he thought is the unchanging psyche or soul that contains non-empirical knowledge remembered from previous life existences. The majority of recalled previous knowledge were the forms or eidos, which were eternal. The eidos were causal patterns of all like things, such as all diverse beautiful things that are linked with the cosmic form of Beauty, and the form of the Even, that link the numbers of two, four and so on. All living things are linked with the cosmic form of Life.

The soul was circularly conceived of by reason as consisting of the ability to reason, to which was subordinated the spirited emotions and the appetitive desires. Plato was mistaken in his conception of the soul as he placed reason as the primary part and function of the soul. In reality, the human soul consists of a triune immanent force of hunger for food, sex and reproduction, and aggression. Reason is but a secondary evolved ability for measuring and calculation.

Greek Soul

The Greek playwright Sophocles (circa 497-406 BCE) exposed to view the human soul through the use of drama in the play *Oedipus at Colonus*. The play was the last written in his life and is more philosophical than his other works. The hero of the play, Oedipus, arrives at Colonus, Sophocles' own birthplace, located near the polis of Athens. Blind from having previously put out his own eyes, Oedipus is led by his two daughters, Antigone and Ismene. In the previous play *Oedipus Rex*, Oedipus unknowingly killed his father and unknowingly married and conceived children with his mother. Oedipus claims that it was moira or fate and he only committed the acts in ignorance, as a lack of knowledge.

Some literary and scholarly critics see Oedipus as a hero near the end of the story as he receives word that he is wanted back in Thebes, the polis he previously ruled and was banished from. However, he dies in a hidden area of a sacred grove. Some critics see these two events as acceptance and forgiveness by the god Zeus. Instead of these intellectual interpretations, dying in the sacred grove can be seen to represent a return to a cosmological force of origin. Oedipus's soul force of sex and reproduction, aggression, and though not mentioned, hunger for food to continue living, is a continuation of a cosmological force. The killing of his father, and having sex with his mother, show the limitation of human reasoning ability, and the primacy of the triune force of the soul, as sex and reproduction, and aggression.

Human ability to reason is frequently perplexed by a feeling of being moved through existence by an unknown force of fate. In reality, the primal force of the soul is a continuation of an unknowing cosmic force. Oedipus, not able to truly know his soul, like most all individuals, suffers through life. Oedipus refers to his situation in life as both fate and a curse.

"Men, guardians of this land, let me tell you who this old man is.
I am an old man tortured by terrible fate."
[The character Thesus says]
"Are you talking about the ancient curse of your family?

[Oedipus answers]
"Not only I, but all of Greece is talking about that curse."
[Oedipus says]
"Friend Theseus, son of Aegeus.
Only gods are free of ageing and death.
All else is in the hands of all-powerful time.
Time changes and reverses all things!
A powerful country becomes weak, once strong a man's body weakens.
Trust lessens and mistrust grows.
Affection fades between friends as between city-states.
Friendship arises between two people but another day turns to hate,
And another day back to love.

So it is my friend, that today relations are well between this country and Thebes,
But time, endless time on its path will bring endless barely tolerable nights,
Nights of warring spears, nights of petty reasons,
To quickly destroy any treaties of peace you have signed with each other...."

Later in the play the chorus speaks:

"Who seeks to live a long life beyond his average span of years
Is plainly a fool.
Happiness evades those who seek a longer life than what the fates
Have assigned as their lot.
One attendant ever awaits at the end,
Hades! Hades waits there for all!
Without ceremony, without dances or songs,
Only death! The end of all is death.
When all is reckoned in, would be better to never have been born.
If born to see the light, the second best is to return to where he came from,
With all possible speed!
A youthful mind thinks not of what pain and suffering will surely come,
Will come betrayal, troubles, arguments, and battles, before the unavoidable end.

Then arrives despised old age, frailness, friendless and lonely,
Abandoned, one's own misery's only friend, is more misery.

Like us Oedipus is old, unhappy Oedipus!
Assaulted like a reef fronting to the north,
Battered all around, by varied tempests tossed,
Unending rain and winds fall upon his head,
Rough relentless waves fall upon him.
From all directions, east, and west,
Waves ever-arrive from sunrise, through midday, and sunset,
As do dark waves from the mountain-shaded sea of the north
To further darken the nights."

These words by Sophocles masterfully portray life and the dynamic forces of the human soul. The individual meets with sudden changes that twist and turn this way and that, through a frustrating maze of existence, ever encountering unplanned and unexpected events that perplex human reason. The statements of Oedipus and the words of the chorus during the play, reflect the philosophical wisdom of Sophocles in story form replete with gods, fate, and a curse. Yet in reality, the real culprit is the human soul as presented in the play. The soul forces are the aggression of Oedipus in killing his father, having sex with his mother and reproduction of children, and to a lesser and not mentioned extent, hunger for food to sustain the strain, struggle, and suffering of life. The soul force is a continuation of not fate but a non-personal, uncaring, cosmological force from which come a lifetime of troubles, helplessness and old age, and finally out of existence by dying and death.

Greek drama is a display of humans making their way through the conscious yet dream-like quality of life situations and attempting to comprehend the unforeseen results of their behaviors. Greek tragedy exposes to human awareness how an individual is limited by reason, and moved primarily by subconscious forces of the psyche or soul through the drama of life. A life of struggle and suffering, and eventually to personal doom of ageing and death. The early Greeks saw life as moved by the forces of capricious human-like gods and irrational moira or fate, all to the mostly no good ends of life stresses, struggles and sufferings. Even the afterlife of Hades (Greek, the unseen) contained struggles, and sufferings.

It is more than coincidence, and also fitting, that the Greek plays portraying tragic life, had their roots in the worship of Dionysus, the god of sex and wine. The name of the god Dionysus is first mentioned by Mycenean Greeks circa 1300-1200 BCE. Dionysus was known by various epithets such as theoenus or "god of wine," khthonios, meaning, god of earth, erikryptos, meaning, hidden one, endendros, he in the tree, and dendrities, he of the trees. His name derived from Greek dios means, of Zeus, and nysus from either the mountain of Nysa where he was said to be born, or from nusa an ancient Greek word for tree.

The worship of Dionysus reveals the human soul to be the triune force of sex and reproduction, hunger for food, and aggression. The imbibing of wine associated with the god Dionysus reduces inhibitions that conceal the psyche or soul within. The exterior practice of worship of Dionysus, more than that of any other deity of humankind, reveals the interior reality of the triune force of the soul. In ritual worship of Dionysus, wine was used to remove any social inhibitions and to induce ecstasy. In the countryside he was worshipped not in temples but in the woods and on the sides of mountains by women called maenads, meaning raving ones. The maenads drank wine, danced, and sang to reach an ecstatic state during which they would engage in uninhibited sexual and aggressive behaviors. Reports mention that animals were chased and when caught, were pulled apart while alive and eaten raw.

The human-like god Dionysus is a symbol for the hidden force of growth within the tree and vine vegetation. He is credited with bringing forth the grape vine and making the first wine. Dionysus is said to be the son of the god Zeus and a human mother by the name of Semele.

Since his father was a god, Dionysus was immortal and also the only Greek god to have a mortal parent. The story is a symbolic way of saying that since the god Zeus was his father and Dionysus was born of a human mother, the sexual force within humans is a continuation of a cosmological force. A cosmological force and a relative triune soul force of hunger for food, sex and reproduction, and aggression, are in reality one and the same.

The yearly festival for the god Dionysus was held in the spring of the year, usually near the end of March, when leaves appeared on the grape vines. The great or city Dionysia festival was led by men drinking wine and dressed in goat skins as satyrs, associated with sexual potency, and carrying a wooden phallus. Accompanied by women the troupe danced, sang dithyrambs, and sacrificed goats to welcome the arrival of the god Dionysus.

The poetic song and spoken choruses were the tragos, the goat song, and the word later gave rise to the word tragedy and the tradition of Greek drama.

The tragedy plays developed out of the worship of the Greek god Dionysus, god of sexuality and his un-inhibiting wine. Under the influence of the alcohol containing wine, the inebriating influence of the god was experienced. Worship of the other Greek gods was experienced mainly through ritual behavior. The greater powerful presence of Dionysus was experienced inside during ecstatic communion of drinking wine and inebriation. The wine facilitated a more intense expression of the human soul force of hunger, sex, and aggression.

Lord of the Flies

To conceive of a human soul as good, and to conceive of something ideal outside of humans as a good human-like god, is to be deluded. The truth of a human soul is revealed by a contemporary literary work entitled, *Lord of the Flies*. The book is consistently rated in many surveys by both readers and editors, to be among the top one hundred books of all time.

The novel was published in the year 1954 by author William Golding (1911-1993). It was his first published book among others written later in his life, and the work won him a Nobel Prize in literature in 1983. Golding was inspired to write his work after reading the book *Coral Island* published in 1858 by the Scottish author R. M. Ballantyne (1825-1894). Ballantyne's book was about three juvenile boys who survived a shipwreck and were marooned on a South Pacific island. On the island they encounter the evils of cannibals, pirates, child sacrifice, tribal gods, and rape. The work has a Christian emphasis with themes of missionary work, repentance, and conversion to Christianity.

The setting of Golding's book also takes place on a deserted island in the Pacific Ocean during an unnamed war. A British plane crashed on the shoreline during an evacuation carrying preadolescent boys away from the evils of war; one group of unacquainted students and the other a religious choir group. No adults survived. On the island the adult instilled thin veneer of civilized reason, and childhood innocence, soon fades away to reveal the primal human soul.

Forced by circumstances to rely on themselves to survive, the student group and the religious group start out by relying on their evolved secondary ability for conscious reasoning. They soon revert to relying on the primal subconscious force of the soul.

The environment though far from the amenities of society, is a rough paradise having fresh water and various fruits and animals to hunt for food. Much of the boys activities are directed to finding food, by gathering fruit and by hunting the wild pigs on the island. In time, the aggression of the hunters led by the leader of the religious group of boys, Jack Merridew, is turned toward the student characters Ralph and Piggy. The boys eventually made a signal fire using Piggy's glasses but the fire, like the boys, turned destructive, and spread out of control burning some of the woods and jungle.

Soon one of the boys tells the others about a snake thing, a "beastie" he had seen in the woods and during the night, and that it wanted to eat him. Eventually, even rational Ralph was convinced of seeing the Beast with teeth and rather big black eyes sitting in one place on the mountain. Eventually the hunters locate and kill a large black and pink sow, whose head was removed and set up on a stick and was soon covered with flies. The story refers to this fly-covered pig's head as Beeezlebub, or Lord of the Flies, hence the book title.

A sensitive boy, Simon, subject to fainting and reverie and in the habit of wandering by himself, walked to the place where the large pig was killed and the guts lay on the ground. Nearby, the removed sow's head was impaled on a pointed upright stick planted in the ground. Simon has a vision in which the fly-covered pig's head, the Lord of the Flies, speaks to him, "Fancy thinking the Beast was something you could hunt or kill…I'm part of you…I am the reason why it's no go…why things are what they are." The evil Beast is revealed to be not outside but inside of humans as "the darkness of man's heart." In reality, the darkness resides not in the heart, but in the triune soul.

The Semitic word ba'al means lord, and refers to a deity that rules to bring or send the living flies that spoil and feed on the death of life. The "Beastly Lord" is what brings a life of sex and reproduction and consequent hunger, aggression, and death into existence.

No outside human-like god has begun the sequence of a life and death struggle. The true ruler is the inside soul force of hunger for food, sex and reproduction, and aggression, as a continuation of a sole uncaring cosmological force.

Golding's story explores the dynamic of what brings the living flies to feed on the dead. For Golding, the beastly cause of existence is inside of humans as two of the triune soul forces that kill for food and kill for aggression. As for the third of the soul force of life, there are no human females present in the story to represent sex. Yet, there is mention of a black and pink sow pig observed to be "sunk in deep maternal bliss" while nursing a row of piglets. The sow pig, the giver of life was killed as were her piglets, and other pigs. The female pig's life and milk-providing body, and her dead fly-attracting head and face, symbolize the true lord of existence. The true lord is the soul force of sex and reproduction that brings life into existence to die by aggression and to be hungrily feasted upon by other life.

Jack was the leader of the religious choir boys, who in the beginning of the story are described as wearing black square caps and black cloaks extending from throat to ankles, and each boy had a long silver cross on the left side of the chest. Even as the choir boys became the aggressive hunters of pigs, and later hunted their fellow boys on the island, no human-like god ever intervened to correct or save the boys. At the end of the story, adults arrive to rescue the boys from the island and each other. For the religious group of boys, the guiding concept of a humanlike god soon fades, replaced by pangs of hunger and emotions of aggression. They answer to no human-like god but only to impersonal nature and the soul forces within.

Golding's work is a masterful metaphorical expose' of the soul of life. Theological stories delude and mask the truth of life by glamorizing a soul inside to be the product of a glamorous human-like god outside. In contrast, Golding's story reveals the truth of existence, that humans are obedient only to nature and to the soul force of hunger for food and aggression, with only a mention of sex and reproduction. Maybe this lesser emphasis on sexuality is derived from proper British etiquette?

Chapter 6

Body is not separate from soul, neither soul from body, yet no man hath ever seen a soul. Rumi

Earth Soul

The theory of Vitalism dates from the 1700-1800's, and has been correctly rejected by modern empirical science. The specious theory states that "living forms come from and contain some vital animating presence that differs from nonliving or inanimate material forms and chemical and physical processes, which do not come from or contain the vital presence." This view is mainly derived from theological religion that the human soul was made by a human-like god out of a special spiritual essence, he breathed into humans to animate the body and to survive physical death.

I would like to resurrect the view of Vitalism by correcting the definition. The view that there is a vital animating force in living forms is correct, while the view that environmental forms do not contain the vital animating force is a false view. In reality, all relative forms are a continuation of a vital cosmological force. From a cosmological force a particle bursts into existence; into boundless space and the support of its cosmic form, which remains tied to it as time. All living forms draw their vitality, their own active movement as an immanent continuation of a cosmological force.

Contact with a vital cosmological force ever exists. Life is a replicating and a self-constructing activity. The vital self movement of life is dependent on non-self movement of the environment. The motion and change of the environment, is dependent on a metaphysical force. Living forms draw vitality from a supporting environment, from consuming other life forms, and as a continuation of a vital cosmological force. Life is the self constructing activity to survive by eating food, having sex and reproduction, and utilizing aggression.

The modern theory of how organic or biological life forms originated from inorganic forms in the natural environment that likely occurred between 4 and 3.5 billion years ago, is known as, abiogenesis. Inorganic molecular compounds exist outside of living forms, as exist in rocks and minerals. A few examples are salts, ammonia, and metals such as copper, gold, lead, mercury, and selenium. These molecular compounds form the basis of chemistry, and do not contain carbon that can bond to the element hydrogen.

In contrast, organic molecules associated with living organisms always contain carbon and also carbon-hydrogen bonds. Organic molecules include lipids, sugars, enzymes, nucleic acids, proteins, and many others. Inorganic or non-living molecular compounds are a supportive necessity for life, while organic molecular compounds are integrally necessary for life. Researchers point out that there is no clear dividing line between inorganic or non-living molecular compounds, and organic molecular compounds of life. Organic life has originated from and is related to inorganic molecular compounds, yet to date there is as yet only a non-comprehensible gradient between the two.

From an aseitical cosmological force, comes related cause and effect animating change that evolves as related living forms of time. From a cosmological force come relative forces, elements of energy, from which comes environment, from the earth comes the chemistry of life. With life comes the relative soul force of hunger for food and eating, sex and reproduction, and aggression.

There are two basic ways of thinking about how life developed from the environment. The first is that life developed terrestrially or on the earth. The second theory is that life developed extra-terrestrially and came to earth from space.

The theory of life developing on earth has variations. The Primordial Soup variation of the theory says that life came into existence based on an early atmosphere, land, and water being stimulated by ultraviolet radiation and/or lightening that produced basic organic molecular compounds. These collected in a primordial soup near shorelines or proximal to deep ocean hydrothermal vents.

Organic complex polymers formed into carbohydrates, sugars, proteins, and eventually self-replicating life.

The theory that life came to earth from space is known as the cosmozoic or panspermia theory. The view states that life exists most everywhere in the cosmos and has spread to the earth, and almost certainly to other planets, via comets, asteroids, and meteorites. Extremophile bacteria survive in debris ejected from life-supporting planets during collisions. Reaching the earth environment of suitable conditions, the bacteria and/or viruses then begin the process of evolution of life forms. Support for the cosmozoic or panspermia theory is that the organic basis for life to exist has been found in places other than earth. In 2010 researchers using the Infrared Telescope Facility in Hawaii, detected water as ice and organic molecules on the surface of an asteroid named, 24 Themis, orbiting between Mars and Jupiter. A meteorite found shortly after impact to the earth in Murchison, Australia, upon examination was found to contain a variety of organic molecules.

Best estimate is that the earth formed 4.6 billion years ago. After this time, self-replicating molecules of life began to develop and evolve on the earth, and then amino acids and proteins. Circa 3.5 billion years ago, simple cell life called prokaryotes evolved, as did stromatolite photosynthesis. Circa two billion years ago more complex cells called eukaryotes evolved and one billion years ago multi-cellular life. Some 600 million years ago animal life evolved, 500 million years fish, 350 million years amphibians, 300 million years reptiles, 200 million years mammals, 150 million years birds, and 120 million years flowers. Approximately 6 million years ago human-like species evolved, and 200,000 years ago modern Homo sapiens sapiens began to evolve to the present day.

Life is fragile. Over ninety-eight percent of species ever documented to live and evolve on the earth are now extinct. Since the earth formed 4.6 billion years ago, at least five mass extinction events have occurred and many lesser extinction events of life have occurred, caused by asteroid and comet impact, climate change, and disease. However, life is resilient, and continues to survive as a continuation of the environment, and as a continuation of a primal cosmological force.

Individual Soul

From an immeasurable and therefore irrational sole cosmic force, comes the soul, a triune force of sex and reproduction, hunger for food, and aggression, relative forces that are also irrational. Physically, the rational cerebral cortex of the brain is supported by the earlier evolved irrational or non-reasoning parts of the midbrain and brain stem. Sigmund Freud in his well-known analogy of the human mind, stated that the conscious Ego that is capable of reasoning is only ten percent, while the other ninety percent known as the Id is unconscious and is therefore not rational.

Each individual does as best they can to consciously manage the subconscious unseen soul force. The irrational soul force, that is, incapable of rational thinking, is often destructive to the individual inside and to others outside. Human conscious reason would prefer a better way. Looking at historical accounts of unreasoning violence of political and religious wars, and the greater and lesser hourly and daily acts of conflict and violence of all kinds small and large, this is just not possible.

Each individual searches for internal and external stability that is never completely and lastingly obtained. Each individual remains in mild, moderate, or intense internal conflict and struggle with the imperative and compelling soul force of hunger, sex, and aggression. Each individual is also in external conflict with the soul force of others. Minute by minute, inside and outside, with oneself and with others, and with time, the individual progresses into situations of struggle, conflict, and suffering.

Seekers of wisdom have realized the precarious condition of life, as well as the problematic heritage of subconscious forces of hunger for food, sex and reproduction, and aggression. Seekers after self and soul comprehension have always intentionally separated themselves from the milieu of social life, as a pre-psychotherapy approach to reduce the internal and external conflict of life. Socially, everyone daily encounters irrational personal situations and people, and observes them in the daily news.

Social experiences distract and hinder individual ability to focus attention and to comprehend. Too much time and effort is required of the average individual to investigate reality experience. Better just to work, consume, reproduce, believe, and take part in rituals of religion.

The unseen cosmological force that moves all things into existence was given a theological makeover of having a human-like personality and thoughts. A god is a way to make the unknown known. To humanize a cosmological force is the shoddy and vulgar work of theologians, religious leaders, and theistic followers. The human-like god that humans worship resides only as a conceived idea in the cerebral cortex.

The will to exist and live resides in the subconscious function of cells and the midbrain instinctual forces for food, sex, and aggression. The human soul is a vital animating force to live, a subconscious willing to exist in living cells and organs of the body. The human soul cannot be observed as an object in space within, but can be observed in a time sequence.

The human soul is active, and consists of both willing and knowing. The soul consists of subconscious willing for food, sex, and aggression, while conscious knowing, functions to better guide the process. Subconscious biological willing evolved cerebral conscious awareness and knowing to be better directed to obtain its needs.

An animating force of life known by the popular term soul, moves living forms in a search for food, sexual acts, and to muscular aggression. That which moves life does so in the direction of death, which is the end of a life of amino acids and proteins, cells and organs but is not the end of what moves it. The subconscious movement of the body is dependent on the movement of the environment, which in turn is dependent on a cosmological force that moves within all things.

All environmental and living forms of existence are embedded in an indestructible field, call it what you will, dark matter, dark energy, or a Bose-Higgs Field.

All originates from an indestructible cosmological force, field, and ground. Therefore, it is suggested that there is an indestructible continuation of it in humans. Inspired individuals like the American poet Walt Whitman and the Persian poet Rumi, aside from poetic sentiment, long ago wrote about an indestructible presence in life forms. Each human triune soul is undying as it is a direct descendent of an undying cosmological sole force that knows not, but ever moves within all.

Pre-scientific View of the Soul

The killing of animals and humans to offer as a sacrifice to a god or forces of nature, is a dim pre-scientific and metaphysical recognition that life contains an animating force. A living body and blood offering to gods or natural forces is a crude recognition that the energy and movement within the physical body is a continuation of a metaphysical force. For the Aztecs of Mexico, the, tonally, or animating force in humans, was in the blood, which became concentrated in the heart when an individual was fearful. The Aztecs thought that without a sacrifice offering of heart and blood, all relative motion would stop, especially daily motion of the sun. By offering the animating life force present in the energetically beating fearful heart and blood of the victim, the Aztec priests prevented the sun from coming to a standstill and causing disorder. How must an Aztec priest have felt to be in the metaphysical presence of that which moved all existence, when he cut and tore the still pulsating bleeding heart from the living human sacrifice? The touching of the blood and heart of the sacrificed animal or human was to directly contact the animating force of life.

Among the Maya, there were twice daily blood-letting rituals, by piercing of the ear, nose, tongue, arms, thighs, leg, and especially the male penis. The blood obtained in this way was used to anoint idols of their gods. The blood obtained from the life-ejaculating penis was thought to have a special animating energetic force that generated the growth of cultivated food plants, especially maize or corn.

There are mentions of the animating life force of blood in bible superstition.

"But flesh with the life thereof, which is the blood thereof, shall ye not eat." (Genesis 9:4) "For the life of the flesh is in the blood." (Leviticus 17:11)

The Christian religion continues this primitive tradition of an animating force. This is evident in the view that Christians are saved through the vicarious atonement of shedding of the blood of Jesus, and the transubstantiation of bread and wine into his body and blood during the Mass. The religion of Islam also practices the offering of body and blood sacrifice of animals to the human-like god Allah during the Hajj, or annual pilgrimage to Mecca, and on other ritual occasions.

The offering of blood or the heart of an animal or human is but the primitive need to get close to, or come in contact with the energetic and essential force of life and existence. Only a barbaric theological human-like god would want the blood and death offering of animal or human. An unknowing cosmological force has no use for offerings of any kind.

Soul Movement

What humans have as a soul is a mysterious ability for cellular and body movement. Everything has an internal movement, from the smallest to the largest, from subatomic particles to galaxies. Life dependently obtains its relative movement from the environment that has an origin from an unseen metaphysical cosmological force. The miracle of movement begins in living cells and organs of the body and continues in conscious willing of behaviors. Metaphysical immanence cannot be observed directly. It can be observed only through conscious observation of its effects as subconscious cellular function, bodily movement, yearning of hunger and desires for food, a strong propensity for aggression, and wanting to continue life through sexual intimacy and reproduction.

Humans move themselves through life with conscious willing and thinking that in turn are supported by subconscious forces of the body, supported by the moving earth and sun, and a greater cosmological force that moves all into, through and out of existence.

The soul is an evolving, coherent relative force, not a special creation of a "once upon a time story" of a human-like god.

A soul is a subconscious organizing ability of cells and organs, and a conscious mind of willing and organizing ability of knowing. No human-like intelligence with a purpose has brought all things into existence. There exists only a blind non-rational cosmological force that imparts momentum.

Existence and human life has not come from a theological rational human-like god but from an irrational cosmological force. A cosmic force is irrational as it cannot be measured or compared with anything. It exists as the immanent and irrational presence inside of humans as the will to exist and live.

A human-like god is the strictly conceptual effort to measure the unknown by comparing it with humans. A human-like god exists nowhere except as a conceived idea originating in the human brain. Conceived and constructed inside the human brain, human-like, is a bridge that extends outside of the brain and across the barrier of an unknown beyond, to end where only a faith-known human-like god is located. The existence of a human-like god is a cognitive delusion, a theological error and deception that humanity has to awake from.

Soul Survival

The triune soul has no size, and easily exists in a single living cell as well as multicellular mammals. Hunger, aggression, sex and reproduction, are considered to be organ specific and hormonal. However, hunger occurs in microorganisms without a midbrain, endocrine system, or digestive tract. In living organisms of viruses, bacteria, and early plants, there is an immanent primal force to reproduce even when not having a midbrain, endocrine system, and genitals. Aggression of pathogenic viruses, bacteria, and protozoa, cause infections and disease, yet lack a midbrain, endocrine system, and muscles.

Western derived Middle Eastern religions insist that only intelligent humans have a soul, and do not accept the view that other less intelligent life forms do.

Yet, while life forms including viruses and bacteria have little capacity for knowledge as compared to humans, there exists a continuation of a cosmological force within them as the will to live. A resilient will to live has been observed in the behaviors of all life forms.

Viruses and bacteria have only a strand or two of DNA or RNA and are the most ancient ancestors of all plants, animals, and humans. A virus is a non-cellular structure of DNA or RNA with a coating of protein and can only grow and reproduce inside a living host cell. Antibiotics do not affect viruses, and antiviral drugs only interfere with their reproduction. Ranging in size from twenty to two hundred-fifty nanometers (billionths of a meter) viruses can be seen only with an electron microscope. A teaspoon of ocean water is a virtual soup of life that by estimate contains a million viruses. Since viruses are not actually living they do not die. Viruses do in a sense die when they infect a host cell and inject their interior DNA or RNA into the bacteria, plant or animal host. All that remains is the exterior protein shell covering of the virus but the dynamic essence of the virus continues to exist through replication, and in this sense they do not die.

Bacteria are single cell living organisms that congregate in colonies or move around individually using flagella. They have rod, round or spiral shapes, and live in soil, water, decaying organic matter, and in and on the bodies of plants and animals. For example, the human body consists of ten trillion human physical cells and one hundred trillion bacteria cells, mostly in the intestinal tract. A teaspoon of soil is estimated to contain one billion bacteria. Bacteria reproduce through binary fission, meaning they divide into another cell, and the new bacterium is an identical clone copy of the original. The average bacterium is larger than viruses measuring about one thousand nanometers.

In the spring of 1958, at a Los Alamos atomic research reactor, physicists looking into the coolant water at the radioactive fuel rods, noticed the water was becoming increasingly cloudy. The water was analyzed and found to contain bacteria of the genus Pseudomonas and when measured was found to contain as many as one billion of them in a quart of reactor water.

The bacteria were sustained by obtaining nourishment from resin and felt filters in the filtration system. It is estimated the bacteria absorbed radiation equal to ten thousand times the level fatal to humans, and under these extremely high levels of radiation, it is theorized the bacteria underwent mutation that enabled them to survive.

In 1995, scientists announced that they had revived ancient bacteria that lived in the intestine of a thirty million year old bee that had gotten trapped and was preserved in tree sap that later hardened to form amber. Research has found that bacteria can survive by slowing down metabolism or by entering a dormant spore mode in which the original cell replicates its chromosome and encloses this copy with a resistant cell wall. During times of environmental stress, bacteria form spores, a dormant thick-walled cell that is capable of surviving for extended periods of time in unfavorable conditions. When conditions become favorable they revive to resume living and reproduction.

During the year 2000, newspapers reported on previously unknown bacterial spores that lived two hundred-fifty million years ago, that were found and revived. The bacteria were isolated in an underground cavern located in the Salado salt formation near Carlsbad, New Mexico. In the cavern, salt crystals formed and bacterial spores were trapped in a small pocket of water in a salt layer at a depth of eighteen hundred feet.

After being transported to the lab under meticulous sterile conditions, the bacteria were extracted from the water and placed onto a growth medium where the spores revived and began to reproduce. Microbiologists were surprised by the finding, as chemically the molecules that make up the structure of the two hundred-fifty million year old spores, now named Bacillus permians, should have degraded long ago.

In 2010 it was reported that bacteria previously sent to the International Space Station for 553 days had been returned to earth. Gloeocapsas bacteria are found in rock cliffs, and sample rocks were transported and placed in containers located on the space station laboratory.

On the space station the bacteria were located outside and exposed to extreme temperatures of day and night. On the sun side of the space station temperatures reached two hundred-fifty degrees Fahrenheit and on the shaded side reached minus two hundred-fifty degrees Fahrenheit. The bacteria were also bombarded by radiation, ultraviolet light, and endured the vacuum of space. Some bacteria in the rock died but many survived to reproduce and to be studied when returned to earth.

What exists in these single cell life forms that enable them to survive? Having an amazing ability to endure and survive, there has to be something more within bacteria than just amino acids and bases of proteins, and the ability to enclose their life function within endospores to survive stressful environments. In bacteria there is little intelligence but there is present a triune soul as hunger, reproduction, and aggression, willing forces to survive as a continuation of a nonperishable cosmological force.

Literature on the Soul

In the Hindu classic, the *Bhagavad Gita*, the god Krishna speaks the words:

"I am the essence of the waters, the shining of the sun and the moon...
It is I who resound in the ether And am strength in man.
I am the sacred smell of the earth, the light of the fire, life of all that lives.
Know me, eternal seed of everything that grows. (Chapter 7)
I am the heat of the sun; And the heat of the fire am I also;
Life eternal and death. I let loose the rain, or withhold it,
I am the cosmos revealed, and its hidden essence." (Chapter 9)

In these words the human-like deity is telling what it is, not a personality but a cosmological force. The enlightened author of the work is giving voice to his own realization and direct perception of the reality of a cosmological force that moves all things into existence, and moves within them as a soul force willing to live.

The American poet Walt Whitman (1819-1892) says in his collection of poems, *Leaves of Grass*:

"A child said, What is the grass? fetching it to me with full hands;
How could I answer the child?...I do not know what it is any more than he.
I guess it must be the flag of my disposition, out of hopeful green stuff woven.
Or I guess it is the handkerchief of the Lord, A scented gift and remembrancer designedly dropped, Bearing the owner's name someway in the corners, that we may see and remark, and say Whose? Or I guess the grass is itself a child...the produced babe of the vegetation.
Or I guess it is a uniform hieroglyphic...Sprouting alike in broad zones and narrow zones...
And now it seems to me the beautiful uncut hair of graves...
I wish I could translate the hints about the dead young men and women...
What do you think has become of the young and old men? What do you think has become of the women and children?
They are alive and well somewhere; The smallest sprouts show there is really no death,
And if ever there was it led forward life, and does not wait at the end to arrest it,
And ceased the moment life appeared. All goes onward and outward...and nothing collapses,
And to die is different from what any one supposed, and luckier."

Commenting on Whitman's poem, the observed grass, and leaves of deciduous trees, and many other plants on the earth shrivel and die during the cold climate of winter. Yet, an immanent invisible force in the roots brings forth new growth when required conditions of temperature, water, and soil nutrients exist.

The existence, growth, and life of grass is rooted in the relative co-conditions of environment necessary for the growth of grass and all of life, and these are further rooted in a greater cosmological force. The visible form withers and dies away but the life force in its roots brings forth season after season the original plant life form and also other living plants through its seeds.

An analogical hint for the dynamic of human existence can be found in plants. The scientific view of life can be compared to annual plants that exist for just one season and then die to only live on through its seeds. The view of western religion can be compared to biennial plants having two plant life seasons, a first year of growth and a second year of more growth and blossoming. The first growing season can be compared to earthly life and the second growing season can be compared to blooming, or withering, in an afterlife. The view of eastern religions and reincarnation can be compared to perennial plants, which can continue to live for twenty seasons or more during which the visible top of the plant may die and not exist but its roots continue to exist in the dark soil and regenerate the visible plant many times during many seasons.

The grass cannot comprehend it is growing, cannot stop growing or stop its growth cycle; as long as conditions are favorable it continues to grow. Animals are conceived, grow, and cannot stop their instinctive sexual reproduction, eating, and aggression.

Humans are conceived, born, grow, eat, behave aggressive, and sexually reproduce, all as a continuation of conditioned motion and change of an environment, and the environment is a continuation of a greater cosmological force. The soul forces of life have their roots not in a human-like god but in an unseen cosmological ground.

Whitman says, that the smallest sprouts show there is no death. Death is an evolutionary change. Similar to a family house there are many rooms, and walking into a house through a doorway, an individual enters into another spatial dimension. The individual can continue on into other rooms of the house, or return to the room from which he began, or exit the house to travel elsewhere.

Chapter 7

The soul is wonderful say fawning fools, empty words of modern times when an excess of stupidity rules.

Triune Soul

Of the triune soul function, it can be argued that as a continuation of a cosmological force, aggression first evolved to localize as relative force and then energy to occupy a space. Second developed a need for energy to grow and increase in size. Third occurred replication and evolution of relative forces and element energies, and environmental forms. This development sequence is mimicked by the cycle of human development, conception of life. Male sperm aggressively compete to fertilize the female egg and to occupy a space, the embryo needs nourishment to grow, and eventually in adolescence puberty develops to reproduce. The triune soul force is an immanent function of human behavior, seeking for food, for sex or providing for the results of reproduction, and seeking ways to be aggressive as competition in work, sports, or violence of crime and wars.

From a sole force comes the soul. One cosmological force is both transcendent and immanent in humans as a triune biological and psychological soul force of hunger for food, sex and reproduction, and aggression. The primary subconscious triune force of the individual soul, easily overwhelms the secondary and later evolved ability of reason and conscious thinking. The forceful urge to have food, sex, or be aggressive, quite easily hijacks the rational processes of reason. It is difficult to think clearly when hungry, when sexually frustrated, and during situations of emotional anger and aggression.

The triune soul is the unnoticed essence and depth of human life, while reason is only the surface overlay. As an iceberg is ten percent above the surface and ninety percent below the surface of the water, so too human conscious awareness is only ten percent, while the triune soul force of hunger, sex, and aggression is ninety percent subconscious.

It is the conscious ten percent of human awareness that conceives and projects a human-like god, as a way to escape from the lower ninety percent of the triune soul force of life.

Rational and Irrational Soul

The word grow is defined as, "to increase in size or quantity through time, to develop or become more complex or mature." What moves and grows the parts of the human body are energy particles of electrons and atoms, as a continuation of a sole cosmological force. From a cosmological force, a continuation exists inside of humans as a triune soul force of hunger for food, sex and reproduction, and aggression. The soul is a force that organizes and evolves the body and the brain. In the universe everything either "goes" or "grows," and all that grows comes from what goes as a cosmological force.

All measurable relative motion is a continuation of an immeasurable force. Modern cosmologists can measure remnant radiation of a Big Bang but not the causal beginning of what brought it into existence. A cosmological beginning is not measurable so is irrational, and only what is measurable is rational. What is measurable are relative phenomena of size including height, width, depth, and a weight occupying a space and motion as time. Relative forces of gravity and magnetism are measurable, as are energy elements, environmental forms, and life is measurable. What is not measurable is not rational.

For historic and contemporary theistic humans, the immeasurable and irrational moving force of the universe is made rational by anthropomorphizing it to be a human-like god. In reality, a cosmological force is an irrational force, as is the triune soul force of hunger for food, sex and reproduction, and aggression. The primary soul force is marginally rational only as mediated by the evolved cerebral cortex of the brain.

Some philosophers and theologians have conceived of the human soul as rational. Christian theologians contributed to the view of a rational soul by utilizing the views of the Greek philosophers Plato (427-347 BCE) and Aristotle (384-322 BCE), and later the scholastic theologian Thomas Aquinas (1225-1274).

For Plato, humans have a tripartite soul, the main and most important part he thought was reason, followed by the lesser yet essential parts of spirited/emotional, and appetitive function. Aristotle thought a soul is what forms living things. He classified plants as having a nutritive soul, animals as having a sensitive soul but only humans as having a rational soul. The medieval Christian theologian Thomas Aquinas thought that since a human soul comes from the goodness of a human-like god, then the essence of the human soul consists of reason and intelligence that is not destructible, and continues to exist after death of the body.

In contrast to these rationally conceived views of the soul as rational, the philosopher Arthur Schopenhauer (1788-1860) advocated that the soul consists of an irrational will that moved not only humans but all phenomena into existence. Sigmund Freud (1856-1939) followed later with his view not of a soul but of the human self as a conscious Ego, a partial conscious and subconscious Superego, and an irrational unconscious Id. In their writings, both Schopenhauer and Freud provide many concrete and convincing examples to support their views.

Following in the irrational tradition, the soul is a continuation of a cosmological force, and consists of the triune force of hunger for food, sex and reproduction, and aggression. The human soul "ain't pretty," as it is perpetually troubling and troubled. Each individual is frequently troubled by hunger and the obtaining of food, by obsessively wanting to have sex and the results thereof, and troubled by a range of aggression from mild annoyance to violence. The soul has not been created by a human-like god, and the soul is not a sparkling light of reason, nor is it a shining place in the physical body.

Though having an evolved brain capacity to reason, calculate, and measure, humans are only partially rational. Statistics of the Center for Disease Control (CDC) show the average combined physical weight of both females and males is 180 pounds. Of this weight the brain weighs approximately three pounds. The cerebral cortex having reasoning and language ability is seventy-five percent of brain weight or thirty-six ounces.

Based on the weight of the unreasoning body and twenty-five percent of the brain, the majority part of the human organism does not reason, is unreasonable and irrational.

Being only partially rational at best, the dynamic behavior of the human soul for food, sex, and aggression, is why a caring human-like god is imagined. Humankind is borderline rational and has sought and continues to seek to be more rational by conceiving of and emphasizing a much more rational human-like god. Human intelligent reasoning and measuring also overemphasizes its importance by conceiving that human reasoning ability came from the intelligence of a human-like god. In reality, a god represents a future potential of humans to better reason. The great fault of humankind is cognitive ignorance, the seeing of a separation of life from the environment, and the separation of both from a cosmological force. The separation occurs by conceiving of a human-like intelligent god and hypostasizing it to be real.

The first human-like analogically conceived presence was the tangible earth viewed by Paleolithic Neanderthal and Homo sapiens sapiens as a mother that gave birth to plants, animals, and humans. Eventually, the Iron Age cultures of the Middle East conceived a first father who was intangible and not visible. The human-like male god never appeared, and only sent events or things from his far away realm of the sky to affect the earth below. The phenomena were strong masculine-like forces such as blowing winds, intense storms of dust or rain, frightening thunder and lightning, lunar and solar eclipses, and comets and asteroids to spectacularly impact the earth. It was thought that only a rational human-like maker of heaven and earth could possibly send or withhold the display of these immense and irrational spectacular events.

A human-like god is a conceptual strategy of making an irrational existence rational. A god is a way of handling sudden unplanned changes that occur to the best of imagined human plans. Irrational humans meet in the imagined presence of a rational human-like god who looks at humans from the outside and serves to guilt or to threaten humans to think rationally. A god is an imagined rational presence to influence humans to be rational with each other.

A rational god is a way of limiting and controlling the irrational human soul.

Tripartite Characteristics

Through the history of human endeavor there have been various efforts to comprehend reality and the human condition through the attribution of tripartite characteristics. This is based upon something other than a fascination with the number three, a triangle shape, and historic tradition.

One of the earliest formulas of a tripartite reality, are the three main gods of Hinduism known as the Trimurti, meaning three forms. The three main gods are Brahma the creator, Vishnu the preserver, and Shiva the destroyer and transformer. Another Indian son, Buddha, spoke of three Insights of existence as impermanence, ill-fit-together and suffering, and not an eternal soul or self. The Chinese philosopher Lao Tzu in verse 67 of the Tao Te Ching spoke of the cosmological force of the Tao as having three attributes of giving, balance, and not wanting to be foremost. The Greek philosopher Heraclitus spoke of the Logos as change, opposition, and balance. The Greek philosopher Plato spoke of the psyche as consisting of reason, emotional/spirited, and as an appetitive function.

Theologians of Middle Eastern religions speak of three characteristics of a human-like male god, omnipotence, omniscience, and omnipresence. Christians further speak of a tripartite Father, Son, and Holy Spirit. In the field of psychology, Sigmund Freud distinguished the personality as Id, Ego, and Super-ego. In modern times the bedraggled New Age movement speaks of a body, mind, and spirit.

The tendency to impose an overlay of tripartite characteristics, or a numerical group of three on reality processes or the human self, suggests awareness of the human brain/mind to impose a sequence of past, present, and future time. The tendency also may be a subliminal unarticulated awareness of three dominant subconscious determinants of animal and human behavior.

The conscious tendency to assemble and to use so many and varied tripartite attributes suggests a subconscious awareness of a triune soul of hunger for food, sex and reproduction, and aggression that enables life to survive.

Hunger

Hunger is a biological and psychological force to ensure individual and species survival. It is a dynamic of a triune soul. Hunger is defined as a, "physical sensation of wanting food." Contractions of stomach muscles produce what are called, hunger pangs that are partially mediated by hormones such as ghrelin and leptin. Children and adolescents often experience more intense hunger pangs. Low levels of glucose in the blood also stimulate a response from the midbrain almond-sized hypothalamus that secretes various related hunger neuro-hormones. Lack or low food intake results in irritability, weakness, lack of concentration, and even light-headedness or dizziness.

Hunger pains result from irritation of the stomach lining when food is not present and the stomach walls rub against each other causing a gnawing sensation that is only relieved when food is ingested to separate the stomach walls again. Hunger is a twin of aggression. The teeth, stomach muscles, hydrochloric stomach acid, and enzymes also aggressively break down ingested foods, as does peristalsis or smooth muscle movement of the intestinal tract.

Sex

Sexual frustration can be defined as, "a condition of an animal or human having symptoms of irritability, moodiness, agitation, stress, anxiety, sleep dysfunction, depression, and aggression, caused by prolonged voluntary or involuntary sexual inactivity or dissatisfaction." At the time of puberty, there is an onset of an intense biological and psychological felt force to have sex. From puberty on, not having sex is the cause of much frustration and aggression. Humans continually deal with their sexuality, with their frustration of not having a partner or having an unsatisfactory partner.

Humans may experience the frustration of attraction and wanting to have sex with someone, fantasize about sex when waking, and during dreams while sleeping.

The need for sex takes individuals into abusive relationships, alcohol and drugs, dysfunction, fetishism, and compensatory substitute behavior of masturbation. Not to have sex results in frustration, anger, and an inability to concentrate. To have regular sex one marries but as time goes by satisfaction wanes and boredom sets in, accompanied by relationship aggression.

More powerful than reason, sex can complicate or ruin relationships. Though reasoning is loath to admit this obvious fact, the primary sexual urge is such a strong biological and psychological force that it affects and can overwhelm conscious knowing, making it difficult to focus attention and to think. Excess sexual force or what Freud called "libido" of the body affects the ability to relax, affects memory and the ability to recall. Not having sex, the individual builds up serum levels of testosterone, even in women but more so in men. Excess testosterone levels can contribute to anxiety disorders in an attempt to control the strong force of sex, and can lead to over-attachment to a partner, jealously, addictive and possessive behavior of fighting, stalking, divorce, rape, incest, abuse, homicide, and suicide.

The intense forceful biological and psychological need for sex and orgasm is not easily denied. Most individuals must have sexual experience to avoid becoming irritable and neurotic. Dynamic sexual force also makes its primal presence felt in erotic dreams and nocturnal emissions.

If an individual is not busy seeking and obtaining sex, then he or she is kept busy caring for the results of sex; pregnancy and children. Sex can intentionally or unintentionally result in reproduction, the pregnancy and birth of children and tiring life toil of caring for the living continuation of the sexual act.

While a child is definitely a joy, the begetting of children also bestows upon them a death sentence. This sentiment is eloquently echoed in the words of a man who was born and lived in Syria.

He is known by many today as Al Ma'arri (973-1057 CE). He became infected with smallpox between the ages of three to five years and the disease so impaired his eyesight that he became blind, perhaps from youth or from middle age to his death at age eighty-four years. He never fathered children, and the following words are inscribed on his tombstone. "This is what my father has brought upon me and I haven't brought upon anyone."

Moderate discipline of sex is good so as to avoid many of the troubles associated with its indulgence. With practice, sexual discipline amps up the energy to the brain sex centers and enables the individual to better focus attention and contributes to enhanced creativity. When through individual discipline the strong urge for sex is reduced, hunger for food is subdued, and aggression toward self and others is removed. The many and varied troubles of social life fade, replaced by peace and ease.

Aggression

Living forms evolved to display an innate cosmological heritage of aggression. The innate immune system is an evolved strategy of aggression found in most life forms. Even single cell bacteria have a rudimentary enzyme defense against viruses. An innate immune system is also present in fungi, plants, multi-cellular organisms, insects, and evolved life forms including humans. Its cell-mediated response is immediate, non-specific, and is the first line of defense against infectious pathogens and other non-self organisms.

In conjunction with the innate immune system, an adaptive or acquired, immune system evolved in vertebrates to provide a specific response to antigens. Antibodies are proteins produced by the acquired immune system that aggressively seek to interrupt and to deactivate foreign substances known as antigens. When an antigen enters the body, it stimulates the immune system to produce antibodies that attach or bind to the antigen to render it inactive. Antigens are usually viruses, bacteria, or fungi that cause infection and disease. Antigens can also be common allergens such as pollen, dust, animal dander, bee stings, or certain foods such as wheat, corn, soy, and others that may stimulate allergic reactions by the immune system.

Following a specific infection and the production of antibodies, and survival, immunity is acquired which is also the basis of modern vaccination or immunization. A condition of immunodeficiency occurs when immune system function is impaired, such as with HIV/AIDS. Having an impaired immune system and acquiring a secondary serious infection can result in the death of the person. Blood transfusions may also contain antigens that differ from those in the recipient's blood and will stimulate the production of antibodies that can cause potentially lethal allergic reactions.

The human digestive tract consists of the organs of the mouth, esophagus, stomach, small intestine, large intestine, and rectum that function to ingest food, aggressively digest it to extract nutrient energy, and expel feces and urine waste products. The length of the gastrointestinal tract of an average adult is twenty-eight feet. Approximately seventy to eighty percent of the human immune system is located in the gastrointestinal tract, where an average of five-hundred different species of bacteria reside. The amount of bacteria in the intestinal tract weigh between two and three pounds. Approximately ninety percent of these bacteria are beneficial while ten percent do not provide any benefit or are harmful.

The challenge for the immune system is to correctly determine differences between good cells of nutrient foods and beneficial bacteria, and harmful bacteria cells and viruses. The ability of the immune system to function properly is influenced by genetics and the ratio of beneficial bacteria to harmful bacteria in the intestine. The immune system must either develop a tolerance to the essentially foreign cells of every ingested food, or to cause an immune response and attempt to aggressively destroy and remove it.

It has been estimated that the human body consists of ten trillion cells while the bacteria cells in the intestine number one hundred trillion. Intestinal bacteria or flora function like a body organ and perform various functions, such as setting tolerance limits for the immune system to respond to only harmful microorganisms, and fermentation and digestion of nutrients.

The intestinal tract of a fetus is sterile. Following birth and soon afterwards, strains of bacteria from the mother through holding and nursing, begin to colonize the infant's intestinal tract. These early bacteria affect the developing immune system to tolerate their own species and also to be aggressive to those of any harmful or competing species. Intestinal tracts of vaginally born infants are colonized and established within a month, while caesarean born infants take up to six months to become established due to a diversity of bacterial strains from the environment. Breast fed babies have a dominance of bifidobacteria while formula fed babies have a more diverse range of bacteria species.

Autoimmune Aggression

A healthy immune system recognizes, attacks, destroys, and "remembers" bacteria, viruses, or any health-threatening agents not normally present in the body. The aggression of the immune system is unfortunately also directed toward the individual's own body cells, tissues, and organs. Conditions known as autoimmune disorders, can develop in which the immune system aggressively attacks the individual's own body tissues and organs.

A defective immune system is one of the most prevalent causes of human disease in modern times, numbering over 160 autoimmune system disorders or related disorders. A dysfunctional immune system can cause harm throughout the individual by directing antibodies against its own tissues. Inflammation is a response of the immune system to injury or infection, and symptoms include redness, swelling, which is caused by an increase of blood flow to the tissue, heat, and pain.

Allergies are also the result of immune system disorder. Allergic symptoms occur when the immune system aggressively responds to exposure of allergens in the environment that enter the body causing symptoms of sneezing, swelling of tissues, redness, and watery eyes, frequently diagnosed as allergies, asthma, and eczema. Subclinical or low-grade inflammation in the body is caused by the immune system response to many factors.

These include air pollution, smoking, poor diet, obesity, stress, sleep deprivation, all of which also contribute to premature ageing and an increased susceptibility to disease. Low level chronic cellular oxidative stress known as para-inflammation is a major cause of degenerative diseases and aging.

Dental plaque consists of bacteria that produce an inflammatory response by the immune system. Plaque and calculus on the base of the teeth irritate and inflame the tissue and can lead to gingivitis or inflammation of the gums, and periodontal disease when the gums and bone recede and no longer hold the teeth in place resulting in tooth loss.

The individual immune system developed cellular and chemical aggression to protect living cells. The immune system response is cell mediated aggression dependently evolved from the environment. Aggression is an innate soul force that is a continuation of a cosmological sole force. From a cosmic force came relative forces of magnetism and gravity to occupy a space, and energy particles of elements to occupy space to the exclusion of other particles and elements. The elements form the environment of stars, planets, moons, comets and asteroids that are often observed to collide with and destroy each other.

Living forms evolved a triune soul to display this innate cosmological heritage of aggression of varying prey and predator species. Life feeds on life. Dead bodies and foods rot as many life forms are aggressively feeding on them, moved by the necessity to survive of a triune soul force of hunger, sex/reproduction, and aggression.

Chapter 8

Meditation leads to an increase of wisdom, not meditating leads to a decrease of wisdom. Buddha

Meditation

That which exudes all forms and withdraws them back again endlessly, the unending one, ever present in the concord and discord of every difference, is one cosmological force. Meditative calming of willing and knowing can touch that to which no words adhere, in which all exists, an untimed essence to which all else is time, the reaching of a quiet joy of comprehension.

A human-like god is a projection of what Freud called the super-ego, the conscience. A human-like rational god is the larger super-ego placed outside by its human creators, conceived in the brain in response to irrational soul forces inside the individual and outside in other humans, and the environment. Through life, both a god and a government are required to observe and correct humans, as they cannot do so themselves. Family, community, and psychotherapists also observe and serve to correct individual behaviors. Humans have difficulty observing and correcting themselves through introspection or, looking within. Meditation disciplines encourage internal observation and discovery of both rational and irrational processes.

The average theist does not meditate but only prays to a human-like god. Directing attention outside and calling on a human-like god during prayer, the individual quiets himself and prays and asks for a response or answer. With attention focused on what is higher outside, personal distractions of memories and imaginations are calmed to allow an answer to arrive. In reality, an answer does not arrive from a god but from the individual's own higher inner intuitive comprehension. The theistic practice of prayer is psychologically superficial when compared with the much older and well- explored depths of Eastern methods and practice of meditation.

When attempting to look within or meditate, the average person encounters a jumble of emotions, memories, imaginations, and associations. Attention is usually impaired by social distractions. Life is a busy experience of obtaining food, sex and reproduction, and avoiding or inflicting aggression. Awareness of the average person is limited to what is outside of them, and usually very limited as to what is inside body and brain. Meditation focuses attention to reduce distraction to outside objects, and to better focus attention through sensing inside experience. Through training of attention there is an increase of proprioception or awareness of body parts, and enhanced distinctness of emotions, memory, imagination, perceptions, and concepts.

Only a minority of the population on earth has ever practiced meditation, so that very few have been able to comprehend what the soul truly is. While a general description of the soul has been offered, such as it is not physical or material, no accurate identification and explanation of what the soul is has been previously and clearly set forth.

Awakening

From ancient times the development of various meditation disciplines have been the supreme accomplishment of India. Of all philosophical-psychological teachings known to humankind, only the individual called the Buddha managed to clearly comprehend what the soul truly is. Yet, even his profound comprehension is indirect and limited by language. The *Dhammapada*, is a collection of sayings accepted by tradition as having been originally spoken by Buddha. However, the document does show evidence of later interpolations. The following two verses are accepted as having been uttered by him at the time of his awakening.

"Through many lives I wandered, seeking but not finding the builder of this house; ill it is to be born again and again. (Verse 153)
House-builder, you are seen, no house shall you build again! Rafters and ridge-pole are dismantled. My mind has reached the unconstructed; all constructing desires now seen to end." (Verse 154)

Buddha saw not just the house or physical body, but also the "builder of the house," of what builds the body. The builder of the house is not a human-like god but a triune soul force as a continuation of a sole cosmic force from which come all things into, through and out of the dimensions of existence. While not plainly stated in the above verses, the constructing desires can only be willing behaviors for food, sex and reproduction, and aggression. Evidence for this assertion can be found in the remedy for these constructing desires, in the ascetic forest-dwelling and later monastic lifestyle. The ascetic lifestyle requires eating of one meal each day before noon, celibacy or no sex and reproduction, and meditative development of compassion to reduce aggression. These practices are a disciplined way of ending the subconscious and conscious soul forces of self construction that direct attention to eating, sex, and aggression.

The Pali word buddha means, awakened, and was originally used as an adjective. The term changed when it began to be used to refer to the individual known as Buddha, the one who reached an awakened or evolved stage of cognitive development. Buddhists agree that waking consciousness is for most everyone, a daily sleep and dreaming as a continuation of nighttime sleep and dreaming. Waking sleep consists of subconscious habit behaviors and thinking, while waking dreams are conscious memories and imaginations of future events that seldom match up with situations unfolding in time. The philosophy and psychology of Buddhism is the meditative effort to better perceive reality.

According to story, Buddha observed that life was subject to disease, ageing, and death. Seeking safety, Buddha observed and perceived that the body is unsafe. Seeking safety, he did not turn to the human generated concept of the gods of the time to be saved, but insisted on observing life and himself more closely for answers to life. After six years of effort, at age thirty-five, he attained to the safety of nirvana, and until his death at around eighty years of age, he taught others how to find safety by the meditative practice of perceiving and comprehending for themselves.

During the fifth full moon month of the lunar year, Buddhists gather in the ritual of Vesak to symbolically share in the original accomplishment of inner and outer perceptual clarity of illumination reached and declared by Siddhartha Gautama. He became known thereafter as Buddha or awakened one. Yet, it is not possible for many to get to a place of inner and outer clarity of perception to comprehend the "builder of the house" or body. Very few are ever able to reach the achievement of reducing inner and outer subconscious and conscious struggle, so as to clearly focus attention and to comprehend.

Meditation Practice

Meditation is the training of the body, conscious attention, and the forces of the soul. Meditation is a fixing of attention on a sound, image, idea, or part of the body. Training of conscious attention calms perception, (the subconscious process to find significance or meaning) and conception as the mainly conscious process of remembering, imagination, association, and reasoning.

Meditation is the practice of calming conscious thinking, and the subconscious soul force of hunger, sex, and aggression. The average person gives up thinking clearly, as it requires meditative effort to reduce distractions and to awake from the sleep-like social fantasies of religion, and the concealing costume of hope and social optimism. A non-meditative individual risks maladjustment, and in frustration struggles against self or others best interest, causing troubles and harm. Many individuals succumb to the instinctual will to live by excelling in eating excess quantities of food, lust for sex and reproduction, and acts of aggression. For only a few does a soft glow of light dawn to illuminate the inner soul process of life, a life that ever moves onward blindly and often frustratingly seeking personal fulfillment.

For the average person an untrained focus of attention is easily distracted and concentration is usually limited to pragmatic tasks such as work, shopping, and chores. Only the individual who pulls away from a busy life is able to investigate.

The average person has neither the ability nor the time to investigate his own mental and physical processes as he is always in the company of family, friends, coworkers, and busy shopping. Being overly sociable distracts from meditatively examining oneself and others. The person then endures trivial details that distract by continual shifting of attention to past, present, and future events. Life becomes one distracting situation after another. Rather than explore and think for oneself, the individual may find shelter and comfort in a social or religious group. Among the members, there occurs association, cooperation, identification, and imitation.

Time spent away from social activity, reduces excessive mental functions of conceptualizing and reasoning. Repetitive distraction of attention becomes cognitive impairment, and the remediation of the distraction of attention can only be accomplished by privacy. Retiring to a quiet or natural setting, is a way to reduce social distractions of overeating, sex and reproduction, and the temptation to verbally or physically inflict aggression.

A meditative focus of attention to a now experience of passing moments, develops along with intuitive perception. In a retreat to nature, social-based conceptions are reduced to reveal more pristine perceptions and sensitivity. Meditative observation calms the brain/mind function of utilizing sensations to make mental images of memory and imagination, and continual making of comparisons and associations. Attention is calmed by natural energy of soil, water, weather, sun, moon, stars, night, and plant and animal life.

Meditation Benefits

The practice of meditation benefits clarity of thinking and creativity. For example, Albert Einstein (1879-1955) practiced a meditative concentration to better comprehend and find solutions in physics. He referred to his meditative discipline as Sitzen Denken, or sitting thinking, the practice of which led to the profound insights of quantum theory.

Meditating on the demands and function of the body, increases awareness of health, and therapeutically removes stress that cause many physical and mental disorders.

An individual pays almost exclusive attention to outside events, and grossly neglects what occurs inside the body, until inevitably pain directs attention to an injured area. Meditation develops the ability to focus attention to better see, so as to sort out the inside jumble of emotions, memories and imaginations, and conceptions that contribute to stress and illness.

Modern society emphasizes conscious reasoning and alertness that rises to a harmful and pathological level by promoting a lifestyle to go and do all day long boosted by caffeinated coffee and energy drinks. Humans become marooned in the waking conscious mind of reasoning, calculating, remembering, imagining, and associating. The individual becomes shut off from entering into a state of natural meditative reverie and touching of subconscious awareness of intuitive and extra-sensory perception (ESP).

Symptoms of a person being marooned in the conscious mind are prolonged stress, and not being able to recall nightly dreams. After a day of toil on the job, the greater majority of the population goes home, eats dinner, does chores, watches television or reads, retires to bed, finally to relax and transition from waking to sleep. Most find it difficult, or do not recall their nightly dreams. For those who do not meditate, there exists only the limited personal reality of either waking sensations or sleep. For the majority of the non-meditating population, focus of attention, concentration, intuition, inspiration, creativity, extra-sensory perception, and the remembering of dreams during sleep, are not a reality and do not exist.

A meditative person also works at a job, comes home, eats dinner, does chores, watches television or reads, but in addition takes time to meditate during the day. The individual who practices meditation does not go from waking to sleep. Instead there develops the ability to descend from the reality of waking sensations through meditation; to focus attention, concentration, intuition, inspiration, creativity, extra-sensory perception, dreams, and finally into sleep.

Waking
Meditative focus of attention
Concentration
Intuition

Inspiration
Creativity
Extra-sensory perception
Dreams
Sleep

Staying alert during meditation, the individual descends through levels of conscious and sub-conscious where he would normally be asleep. Meditation is not a waste of time. The practice deserves to be made part of an individual lifestyle that is done every day, like eating food or the brushing of teeth.

The practice of meditation reduces stress, develops sensitivity, enhances perception, and comprehension of personal existence. During meditation the individual may also come to clearly observe the mental activity of imagining a human-like god. The meditator may spontaneously and occasionally sense he is connected with the awesome and sublime forces of the environment, and beyond to a cosmological force. On a subconscious level each human knows, though vaguely, they are both time and the time-maker of the cosmic panorama of days and nights, and changing seasons. How can a mere story of a human-like god of theistic religion be superior to an all-moving presence, the ever-flowing of environmental and living forms, into and out of the earthly dimension of existence?

Meditatively observing the parts of the body and its functions leads to the sensing of energy and force contained therein, and that these forces are related or relative to something. Through aesthetic proprioception and interoception, the body and its parts are sensed and intuitively perceived to be related, not to the intruding theological concept of a human-like god but to a cosmological force.

Meditation on the Soul

Human knowledge predominantly consists of the letters of words and numbers that are but surface markers upon a cosmic deep. Words and numbers are in reality only a surface overlay of a reality of forces and energies.

All outward appearing environmental and living forms are constructed of inward energy of elements composed of atoms and electrons as a momentum and continuation of a cosmological force. To approach the truth of a cosmological force, all conceiving and word imagining of a human-like god must cease, and attempts at observation and measurement of science must fall away. Meditative focus enables an individual to perceive and comprehend what the soul truly is. As an individual makes his way through a maze of conscious conceptions to reach a focus of attention, he may gradually perceive subconscious soul functions that transcend the body.

Just as a cosmological force cannot be observed or measured, so too the soul of a living form cannot be directly perceived, only observed to be a dynamic triune force of hunger for food, sex and reproduction, and aggression. Humans through history have not perceived a soul but only wrongly conceived it to be their own personality or ego that remarkably fits quite well with the human conceived ego of a human-like god.

Soteriological Meditation

The soul force of hunger ingests nourishment and water to build parts, sex reproduces parts, and aggression obtains and protects parts. What fits life together is a surrounding cosmological force and a continuation of it as an immanent force. What fits the parts of life together is a continuation of the forces of the environment, and what fits the parts of the environment together is the related energy of elements, forces of electromagnetism and gravity, and a strong and weak nuclear force. What fits all related parts of the environment and life together is a cosmological force.

Life is the movement and function of cells. In plants there is an immanent continuation of force in the silent growth of cells, in animals and humans in the silent growth of hair, toenails and fingernails, function of organs, and the healing repair of injuries. The will to live, to be something, to resist not to be nothing continues as forceful struggle of inanimate and animate forms. Meditation practice is a path of evolving away from the ancient behaviors of earthly struggle.

Humans have evolved from the natural environment, are sexually conceived, and are born into the dimension of the natural earth environment. Based on anecdotal and case study evidence of near-death experiences, and nearing-death case studies, humans will naturally transition into another natural dimension at the time of physical death. An imaginary human-like god plays no part in this reality process. The male and female body and immanent triune soul force brings life and death into existence, as a continuation of a sole indestructible cosmological force.

When young it is easy to think that life will last forever, but eventually dawns the disquieting awareness, that each is just a temporary tenet in the house of time. All humans grow old but few grow wise, and just as few take time to touch the timeless. Reducing the experience of relative time is what the practice of meditation is about. Time is change and is also the transition and link or tie to other dimensions of existence.

The physical human body of a lifetime arrives at the time of death, yet the energy and the forces that move the body do not reach a complete end of time. A subconscious triune soul force that moves the body and conscious thoughts, no longer remains tied to the body lifetime, but does remain tied as a continuation of a sole timeless cosmological force that intersects with and across other dimensions of existence. Surrounded and supported by an indestructible cosmological force, a lifetime pattern of a soul force continues into another dimensional reality or may return to continue life again.

A meditative person sees the wretchedness of life. He then seeks to remedy his precarious condition through the discipline of meditation. Salvation consists of individual effort to comprehend the way out of the omnipotent flow of nature from a cosmological force, as continued in relative energies of elements, the environment, and the triune soul inside living forms. Deliverance is to comprehend that no theological human-like god exists in an earthly dimension or another dimension of the universe. Only the practice of meditative transcendence can save, by clearing the swirling of conscious and subconscious obsessions of an earthly life, to focus attention and to meditatively explore what exists both inside and outside.

Meditation practice is all about a focus of attention, so as to still the subject-object division. Just as quantum particles can be both local and nonlocal, in meditation, attention can be focused so as to experience non-locality. A cosmological force is a surrounding field with which all is interconnected and entangled. As a continuation of a non-local field, meditative awareness can sense the forces of intentions and emotions of others, and this is a basis for extra-sensory perception (ESP).

Meditation is a gradual training of the focus of attention to remove distraction by disassociating from immediate sensory experience of seeing, hearing, smelling, tasting, and touching. With practice, there develops a further focus of attention to exclude mental images, and representations of memory and imagination. With practice, an individual is able to keep a focus of attention for extended moments of time. During the seclusion of meditation, an individual may eventually become aware of three physical and mental forces that distract his ability to focus attention. This is a direct encounter with the will to live as the triune soul force of hunger, sex, and aggression. He respectively makes peace with and guides the soul force toward quiescence, to peace and calm that surpasses all understanding, to nirvana.

Through the diligent practice of meditation an individual comes to find that life does not only consist of conscious attention to now events. During meditation often comes conscious awareness of long forgotten memories of childhood from the present life time, and with continuing practice, memories of past life times are spontaneously recalled.

With an increase of skill in the focus of attention and meditation, for some individuals, the soul force may be found to extend to memory beyond present life experience, found to have roots extending to another life or lives. What moves the series of lives is found to be a soul force that in turn is experienced to be a continuation of a cosmological force that moves all.

Living a life devoted to meditation practice, an individual may eventually come to consciously perceive the subconscious force of hunger, sex, and aggression, to be the long sought soul of humankind. Eventually an individual may find his way to the summum bonum, the numinous and ineffable transcendence of existence.

Chapter 9

Religions are the offspring of ignorance who do not long survive their mother. Arthur Schopenhauer

Time

An all-pervading cosmological force is the origin of time, eternally contrasts relative time events, and is where time ends. Space and time are physical limitations of existence that early humans, in various ways, have sought to physically and psychologically transcend. Gradually evolving and finding themselves in a vast space-time reality, humans developed ways to transcend space and time. To transcend physical limitations of space and time, humans domesticated horses, camels, and llamas, built wheeled wagons, boats, ships, trains, planes, and automobiles.

Psychologically, extra-sensory perception (ESP) developed as a way of transcending space and time. Marooned in a time sequence of change, it was a survival advantage to know what came next. The autonomic nervous system and various plexuses, including the intestinal tract, endowed with billions of neurons, bestowed the subconscious gut feeling, and the ability for extra-sensory perception of revelatory images via the conscious cerebral cortex. Extra-sensory perception is an ability of heightened sensing, and it developed as a way of reducing limitations of space and time based on the need to know and to survive in the environment.

Various ESP abilities of telepathy, clairvoyance, and precognition of future events developed as a way of sensing dangerous animals, threatening weather, and empathetically sensing other humans. These experiences occur during waking awareness and in vivid dreams. ESP sensing also contributed to the ability to find water, find and harvest plants and hunt animals for food, and to find and use ethno-botanical healing plants as medicines.

Directing attention introspectively to find how space and time are an innate cognitive function is a disciplined effort.

In India, the body discipline of yoga and the practice of Hindu and Buddhist meditation developed a way of reducing the limitations of space and time existence through developing the extra-sensory ability of siddhis and abhinnas. Through meditation, Hindus and Buddhists also comprehended the law of relative cause and effect change of karma that moves all through a space and time sequence.

Magic is also a human effort to abolish isolation in space and time, and to go beyond physical limitations by affecting situations, animals, and humans. Early humans in the self-help tradition developed magic in an attempt to influence or cause a good effect, to ward off, or to inflict or cause a bad or evil effect. Magic is the individual willing focus of attention to touch another, to join with them as one, with the intention to influence the other willing person, object or event. Magic is an individual effort and is usually not social.

In contrast to individual skilled practices of extra-sensory perception and magic, the unskilled social concept of a human-like god eventually developed. Accepting the imaginary view of a god, the individual then directed attention to the origin of the space-time environment and life, and beseeched the god to intervene and control events occurring therein. For the mass of humankind, holding the view of a human-like god who can control events occurring in space and time, is a vicarious and easier yet deluded way to navigate through life.

The difficult times of existence is overwhelming for many and most find a compromise way to contend with events. Developed through the years, many seek refuge in the shared view of a human-like god for the purpose of better surviving life and death. A god is a way of not being alone in a vast space and time, and of being safe in an unsafe life and death existence. Many millions of human cares and sorrows brought about and evolved the human-like model of a god that could observe all of space and time. The imaginary god is said to intervene if humans only make offerings and seek help through petitionary prayer.

The Jewish-Christian-Islamic view is that time had a beginning created by an infinite and timeless human-like god, and that time will end and/or be renewed with the final or last judgment by the god. But this is only a human way of comprehending time and a way to promote an ethic of good behavior.

Cosmic Time

The sun and clouds move and change daily across a vast blue sky, and nightly stars, planets, moons, comets, and asteroids of light move across a vast cosmic space of darkness. The vast day and night sky may well be the subconscious inspiration for a timeless and unchanging reality

All that has a beginning and end is a continuation of what is beginningless and endless. All changes as time, as all is tied to a cosmological force that moves all things. All is rooted in what cannot be observed to change, and yet it extends into changing environmental and living forms. With every moment of time, humans are surrounded and touched by endless time. What is in time is tied to the timeless, and what changes is connected with the changeless.

Humans are tied to three dimensions of height, width, and depth, and the fourth dimension of change as time. Things of time do not exhaust the timeless, and things as a continuation of the timeless never become disconnected from it. The timeless does not let what is tied and related to it as relative time become nothing or completely untied from it.

Views of Time

There are two main views of time. One is that time is an objective structure of the cosmos in which event change occurs in sequence. Isaac Newton (1642-1726) thought space and time were objective and absolute realities. For physicist Albert Einstein (1879-1955) time is objective and relative, and he has been quoted as saying, "...for us physicists believe the separation between past, present, and future is only an illusion, although a convincing one."

The other view is that time is subjective and is an a priori function of the brain/mind that along with space and number organizes sensations into a sequence of images of past, present, and future. In Western Europe, the philosopher Immanuel Kant (1724-1804) convincingly discussed his view that space and time are an a priori construct of the human brain/mind, and that space and time do not exist objectively but are the subjective way of representing phenomena. For Kant, time and space are not empirical concepts but are a priori intuitions of a brain/mind that comprehends and represents sense experience though inner images of outer phenomena. Measuring space quantifies extension and distance between objects, and time is a measure used to quantify the duration of objects and motion between them.

Space is an area not occupied or filled with matter. It is a field or ground of an unseen cosmological force from which a tide of relative forces, energy particles, and environmental and living forms flow as a wave, and ebb in return. Time is relative forms extended in space. Objectively, time is numerous relative extended particles and forms that have come from a primal cosmological force whose phenomenal form is space.

Time occurs in space, therefore time is a continuation of a cosmological force that appears as space. Each and every thing is related, and is as modern physics states, interconnected and entangled. For a relative formation to be external to an originating source, it must be tied to it as time and occupy space. To be in space, a relative form must be a time tied to an originating force. Environmental and living forms change and age, as all is in an orderly sequence extending from a metaphysical force into relative change of energy, environmental, and cellular life forms. What is relative is tied to its origin, and has to occupy a space, and so space and time are space-time.

Time is a sequence of change of relative parts that are tied to a timeless all-pervading cosmological force. Humans cannot be untied or disunited from their cosmic origin, so life submits to that force which moves from outside and inside, and to the relative cause and effect change among a plurality of parts.

In both linear and cyclical concepts, all is stuck in time as all is tied to what it comes from, not a human-like god but from a cosmological force. Innumerable measurable relative forms come from and are supported by an unmeasured one. Humans have also poetically expressed views of both eternity and time. "One yearned and moved to part and from the part a yearning for others. From one yearning came separation and difference as affinity and opposition and strife. From one yearning came separation, and came yearning for circular return to oneness."

Time is what living forms are and what they are related to, as they are tied to the environment, which is tied to elements of energy as atoms and electrons, in turn tied to relative forces, which are all tied to a greater cosmological force. Humans observe that in the outside environment, everything changes as motion and time. Wanting to control the motion of the universe, and wanting the origin of cause and effect to care, has in human thinking conceived and produced a collective theological delusion of a human-like god. The imaginary model of a human-like god is utilized to emphasize reward and punishment ethics. In reality, ethics is better served by comprehending that each shares a continuation of a cosmological force that moves all; none are excluded.

As a continuation of environmental change and strife, the heritage of human life is an irrational struggle and strife. Individuals and species are in competitive strife and struggle between the weak and strong. Humankind has only recently observed the evidence for and accepted the reality of environmental and biological evolution as validated by Charles Darwin (1809-1882). All evolves through time, including the environment and life. Life forms are relative to the time of the environment that are relative to elements of energy that are tied to a timeless cosmological force.

Lifetime Goal

The goal of life is to realize the reality of what moves the universe and how humans are related to it. Human genealogical heritage can be traced not to a theological human-like god but to a cosmological force.

However difficult to comprehend, a cosmological force as the origin of relative motion of all that exists, is what truly deserves to be known. The challenge for humankind and for an individual is to glimpse the movement and function of life as a continuation of the moving environment, as a continuation of moving energies and forces, and all as a continuation of a cosmological force.

A cosmological force outside is continued in humans as the subconscious and conscious phenomenon of willing to live, as hunger for food, sex, and aggression. Both religion and science fail to see and acknowledge that human subconscious and conscious willing is a metaphysical function that has an origin in and can be traced to a greater cosmological force. Humans are said by both religion and government to have a free will, yet science insists there is no evidence for a free will. While willing is not free of conditions, humans have a limited ability to will as is evident that an individual may be willing or unwilling to engage in one behavior or another.

Average human thinking is a jumble of thoughts and emotions, associations, memories, imaginations, and is not capable of clear perception and comprehension of how the function of a living physical form can be a continuation of a cosmological origin. A cosmological force from which the environment and life comes from cannot be perceived outside, and is not perceived inside as subconscious cellular function and body growth, and as a triune soul force of hunger, sex, and aggression.

Through limitless beginnings, a cosmological force has ever parted into separate moving parts of related forces, relative motion of energy elements, and environmental and living forms. Instead of sensing an interrelated continuous super animistic force moving all, attention is turned to comprehending objects and forms separate in space and time.

An observant individual, sensing the continuation of a cosmic force in his own willing and doing, seeks to discipline poise in the habits of eating, desires for sex, and the strong willful emotions of aggression. Some few individuals on the earth have perceived a cosmological immanence within themselves, and have taught this to others.

Everywhere a cosmic force ever brings forth; a cosmological force beginningless and endless, which opposes nothingness or oblivion. All that exists is moved by a cosmological force that brims forth relative forces and energies of the environment and living forms. A singular cosmological force brings forth all individual things that in turn actively oppose and struggle against each other.

Just as modern humans look at tribal animistic, magical, and superstitious thinking and behavior as silly and primitive; so will those humans of a future time look at theistic thinking and behavior of a human-like god as a silly and primitive view. Anyone who cannot intuitively perceive a single cosmological force and the continuation of it as three numinous forces of the human soul will be considered to be perceptually primitive and/or cognitively handicapped.

Chapter 10

The boundary condition of the universe is that it has no boundary.
Stephen Hawking

Dimensions of Reality

One air surrounds the earth and enters inside of all living forms to vivify them. Just as there exists one air, so in reality, there can be inferred that one cosmological force surrounds and contains the relative universe of millions of suns and planets, and on the earth, enters into living forms as an immanent force to vivify them. The human soul consists of a triune force that is a continuation of and is rooted in an indestructible cosmological force, ground, or field.

Modern researchers, including parapsychologists, have investigated but to date have not actually found a soul as a measurable thing or object. The failure of this effort is due to a lack of perception and comprehension. What is most active in living forms that insure survival is an immanent biological and psychological force of hunger, sex and reproduction, and aggression, that through accumulated experience stores memory and habit identity of a soul. Human conscious thoughts, emotions, and behaviors, are directed mainly by three primary subconscious forces. These are rooted in and are a continuation of an unseen non-conscious cosmological force, super-positioned and shared by all. For an individual, there exists always a continuity with the environment and others, ever tied to each other directly and indirectly, sharing a cosmological force immanent in all.

Habit Soul

Habits are a clue to the human soul. Habit may be defined as, "An acquired pattern of subconscious and involuntary behavior, a tendency or disposition." Habits are repetitive subconscious memory and behaviors. For example, I moved a table in my house, and for three months when about to place something on it as I was used to, I went to the previous older location of the table, which much to my annoyance was no longer there.

Time after time this happened until the habit formed of going to the new location. The same happened with a tube of toothpaste kept in a location in a medicine cabinet, when I moved the toothpaste tube to a shelf in the bathroom where I kept other items. For approximately two months with occasional instances extending to five months, I looked to retrieve the toothpaste tube from the previous location. As Homer Simpson might comment, "Doh!"

Habits are repetitive subconscious behaviors. When a person consciously practices some behavior such as learning a language, or target shooting, the individual is developing a good habit to perform in a skilled way. Just as various good and bad habits develop and are often difficult to remove, so too the subconscious habits of eating food, sex and reproduction, and aggression continue to exist, not only for a biological lifetime but may continue as a triune soul force of repeating lifetimes.

The triune force of sex and reproduction, hunger and aggression as expressed in a human body is a continuation of a field of related environmental energies and forces all coming from a singular cosmological force, perhaps what is known as dark matter, dark energy, or a Bose-Higgs field, or even beyond these. Physiological functions and behaviors of the body are biological subconscious habits. Since all is embedded in a cosmological field or ground, subconscious habits can and do continue and/or recur. There is much historical and contemporary evidence based on anecdotal accounts of survival such as near-death experiences and after-death visits. There is scientific conducted research of talented mediums that convincingly suggest evidence of survival. There are also many cases suggestive of survival and reincarnation, especially as investigated by the psychiatrist Ian Stevenson and his fellow researchers.

In his research, Dr. Ian Stevenson (1918-2007) (*Children Who remember Previous Lives, 1987*) found that in certain case studies of young children, past life memories are recalled as images, and in other case studies, only past life behaviors are spontaneously acted out.

The conscious personality is a secondary function of a primary soul force of hunger, sex, and aggression experiences stored as memory and usually not subject to conscious recall but expressed as subconscious habitual behaviors. The soul continues as subconscious habitual behaviors into another dimension or returns to an earthly dimension. A human-like god will not save humans but a cosmological force both beyond and immanent in nature will save them to continue in another natural dimension or to return to earth.

Sigmund Freud (1856-1939) the Austrian founder of psychoanalyst, has pointed out that personality is like an iceberg, ninety percent is underwater and only ten percent above the surface. Analogically, just like an iceberg so the human personality is ninety percent subconscious while only ten percent is conscious. Freud posited traumatic memories of deprivation and excesses of sexuality and aggression in the subconscious or unconscious Id that he thought continued to exert an influence until made conscious through psychoanalytic therapy. In reality, the traumatic subconscious memories are secondary effects of a primal subconscious soul force of hunger, sex and reproduction, and aggression.

Freud first began uncovering individual subconscious childhood memories through hypnosis but later developed the free-association technique. Today Brain Weiss, MD (1944-present) and other reputable researchers have used hypnosis to better explore the content of the subconscious and have discovered memories of trauma and experience from previous lives. These "other" subconscious memories were overlooked by Freud and are located in the physical body, yet embedded in the subconscious force of the soul. Freud did not accurately perceive nor properly comprehend what he considered to be only physiological instincts of hunger for food, sex and reproduction, and aggression. Consequently, he did not recognize these dynamic processes for what they are in reality, a triune force of a metaphysical soul.

Soul Save

The will to survive is the essence of life, and should not be under estimated.

The will to live is the effort of obtaining food, a mate for sex or reproduction, and aggressive strength to accomplish both. The will to survive is both involuntary and voluntary. Humans have accomplished amazing feats of surviving accidents and deprivation.

In 2003, to avoid death, a twenty-eight year old rock climber in the state of Utah, amputated his own right hand that had become pinned under a rock for five days. There are many anecdotal reports of animals caught in traps and gnawing a foot off to escape. In 2006 in Indonesia, a female Sumatran tiger was caught in a poacher's steel trap, and gnawed off its right front foot. There exist many anecdotal reports of dogs and cats finding their way home and surviving over hundreds of miles of unfamiliar geography.

Everything in the visible and invisible universe and dimensions, is going and growing. What began this relative motion of the environment and life? Not a human-like god but a cosmological force constructs and organizes the elements and forms of the environment, and as an immanent triune soul force constructs and organizes living forms. The miracle of the motion of the environment is based on a cosmological force, and a continuation of it exists in living forms as the motion and growth of living cells, organs, and bodily behaviors.

The immanent force inside of living growing forms, has its roots in a cosmological force that ever exists. All is rooted in a cosmological force, and an immanent continuation of it exists as a subconscious soul force inside living cells, organs, and as a conscious willing to live of emotions, thoughts, and behaviors. That which fills the subconscious cells of the body with an ache, and floods conscious attention with longing, is the soul force of hunger, sex, and aggression.

A sole cosmological force constructs relative forces of gravity, electromagnetism, and strong and weak nuclear forces, relative energy particles of the elements, and constructs a triune soul force. The triune soul force to exist and survive, constructs and organizes and evolves cells and organs of living forms. Life is a soul behavior of construction, a willing to exist and survive by obtaining food, sex and reproduction, and aggression.

The triune soul force constructs biological life to survive. When an individual dies, subconscious memories and habitual soul force of hunger, sex, and aggression, continue to construct the individual. Just as the soul force of the body organizes and repairs cells and organs, so the soul force repairs the damage of physical death by continuing in another dimension or reincarnating. At the quantum level, forces and particles are super-positioned, and soul forces can shift states to exist inter-dimensionally.

When an individual dies, subconscious memory and habits are forces that self construct. The immanent soul force of cell life, repairs injury to the body by the constructing process of healing growth. What repairs the body is not the conscious self of knowing and personality but the subconscious soul force to live and survive. The soul force retires from the body to continue existence and to repeat through time and other dimensional space.

In the twentieth century psychologists began to appear on the scene, and rather than use the religious term soul, began to use and popularize the word self, meaning "conscious knowing, identity, individual character, personality, attitudes, abilities, behaviors, mental and emotional traits." The word self, is from Old English, selfa or seolf, (German selb, and Old Norse sjalfr). In modern psychology, the word self, has completely replaced use of the word soul. The word self refers to conscious willing and knowing, and character and personality, while soul refers to the subconscious force that constructs, repairs, and survives.

The soul is what moves the body to survive and what survives physical death. The soul, (Old English, sawol, Old Norse, sala, Old High German, seula) is said to be a spiritual (spiritus, Latin for breath, spirare, to breathe) part of a person, which is a misnomer, as the soul has nothing to do with the breath or breathing. The soul is the vital force of life, and at the time of death separates from the physical body, to super-position and can exist inter-dimensionally. A sole cosmological force constructs the soul triune force that constructs and organizes the combined subconscious and conscious self. Life is a constructing activity of survival, repairing of injuries, replicating and reproducing, and even repeating.

As a continuation of a cosmological force, an immanent soul force as the will to live of hunger for food, sex and reproduction, and aggression, constructs the subconscious cells of the body, and in turn evolves and constructs conscious knowing of perceptions, conceptions, associations, memories, and imaginations. In reality, humans no longer need a human-like god as an explanation for life.

Yet, humans want to be saved from the troubles of life and from troubling death, and a human-like god acts for humans on their behalf to save them. In reality, to want one's soul to be saved is to want the individual primary force of hunger, sex, and aggression, to survive. Secondary to soul survival is wanting to have relationships continue or not continue, possessions, abilities and skills, and knowledge. Each wants their individual jumble of primary subconscious and secondary conscious willing forces to continue.

Humans also and mostly want their ability for knowing, to be saved and to endure. Knowing comes through the senses and sensations of seeing, hearing, smell, taste, and touch, that rapidly change second to second. Individual knowing of perceptions and conceptions are accurate and some are distorted and erroneous. Memory consists of happiness and pleasure, and sadness and painfulness. Imaginations of the future are often fulfilling yet just as many are disappointing. For the vast majority, knowing is limited and attention is directed mostly to pragmatic tasks. Many are undereducated, and many more do not meditate and focus attention to observe and sort through the personal jumble of knowing that they so much want to continue to exist. In reality, a human-like god is superfluous, and is not needed to save human life. The soul forces self-construct, and the cosmos has a default save.

Default Soul Save

Science likes to control an uncontrollable existence by observing and measuring, and predicting, and shies away from experiential and anecdotal reports. Science insists on being privy to observation and measurement, and is justifiably critical of historical abuses of blind faith and the many superstitions of religion. However, human existential experience, discounting ignorance and superstition, is in a way, more advanced than science through the prevalent and many anecdotal reports of near-death experience, childhood reports of reincarnation memories, and contact with the deceased, and extra-sensory perception. Trained researchers have lately begun to investigate these long reported areas of human experience, some of which convincingly point to the existence of other dimensional realties. Humankind has not fully appreciated that life on earth is a dimension of existence, and that where one dimension exists, others are probable.

A cosmological force can from the quantum level construct and deconstruct human lives, and at the time of death, it can transform and cloak the soul, and shuffle it off to varying separate yet interconnected dimensions of existence. Once born as a continuation of a sole cosmological force, an individual soul force cannot be destroyed, only resolved. Through a cosmic cause and effect option, the soul is automatically saved at the time of physical death. The universe saves as a default option; each cannot help but be saved and each is doomed to be saved. The real problem of existence is not how to be saved, said to be possible only by a human-like god, but how to reset the cosmic default switch from an earthly save to a progressive cosmic evolution.

The science of physics' empirically verified second law of thermodynamics, known as, the law of conservation of energy, states, "the total energy of a closed system cannot be created or destroyed but changes and is conserved over time." Since a relative soul force is a continuation of a sole cosmological force, it is only relatively destructible and is conserved through time changes.

In contrast, the theological view says that humans must be absolved and saved from intentional destruction by a human-like god. For theistic religions, salvation is defined as that "which brings about the preservation of the soul, to escape from destruction or evil." In theistic thinking, only the greater ego of a god can save the lesser ineffectual ego of his created humans. This is an illogical theistic threat and a symptom of impaired thinking.

The problem of existence is not how to save one's soul, or as theological religion dogmatically asserts, how to have a human-like god save the soul.

The real problem of life is to resolve and reduce the soul to quiescence so as to prevent it from recurrence or reincarnating. The reward sought to attain is to not exist again, at least in biological form. The soul is not something to be cherished and saved as in Western theology, but something to be overcome and resolved as the root of existence. What theological religion values as a wonderful divine soul worth saving for a wonderful divine human-like god, is revealed to consist of a triune force of hunger for food, sex and reproduction, and aggression.

The philosophies of India have known the truth of reincarnation for a few thousand years. The Middle East religions of Judaism, Christianity, and Islam, are antithetical to the view of reincarnation as the process relies on cause and effect karma and is not under the control of a parental human-like god. The Middle East religions also have the primitive, immature, and embarrassing view that the physical body is the real person and that only a god can resurrect it.

Humans are saved in their transition from life to death not by a human-like god but by having a soul that is a continuation of a sole cosmological force. The soul within humans is the triune force of hunger, sex and reproduction, and aggression that enable the individual to physically survive. The soul force that enables physical survival, also enables and ensures metaphysical survival after death.

A human-like god is only the wished for human ability to endure life and to exist beyond death. Humans die and gods don't die, so a god is a symbol for not dying, of continuing on in existence and humans can share in this ability, if the god judges them to be worthy. If a god continues to exist, humans can also.

All that consists of parts departs. All things consist of parts that wear and abrade against each other, and degrade with time. Environmental and life forms are composed of parts and ever smaller parts of elements traced to relative forces and these to a pure cosmological force. What departs the living body at the time of death is the soul, a triune force of hunger, sex, and aggression.

The light of reason attempts to direct and be at peace with the forces of the soul in which it is rooted. Theistic reasoning conceives of that from which humans have come, to be an ultra-reasoning human-like god that resides unseen in another dimension. Since the god is said to be unknowable, then a non-seeing human faith is required.

In the Jewish Garden of Eden myth, the Tree of Knowledge of Good and Evil fruit made by a human-like god, is a symbol for human conscious reasoning and its byproduct knowledge. In reality, human evolved conscious reasoning is inadequate to regulate the unreasoning subconscious triune soul force that is a continuation of a sole cosmological force. The triune soul is a continuation of a cosmic force, not a human-like god. From an unreasoning cosmological force came the unreasoning soul force that evolved the impaired conscious reasoning of humans.

Paradigm

A paradigm is defined as a "basic assumption, a patterned way of thinking, and a worldview that supports a theory or methodology." For some considerable length of historic time, humans have made basic assumptions and developed a patterned way of comprehending how the environment and life came into existence. The early paradigm has long been that the environment and life was made by a human-like god that began existence, oversees it, and waits at the end of life. The god has also variously made a living being out of soil, air, and bone.

In the paradigm of modern physics, quantum super-positioning is defined as, "A fundamental principle that a system or whole compounded of relative fields, parts, or particles, exists partially in many possible states or properties simultaneously but when observed or measured appears in only one of its possible configurations or states." A cosmological force is super-positioned beyond all related forces, quantum energies, and environmental and living forms. A cosmic force is also super-positioned as an immanent force in humans.

Modern science has not been able to observe, measure, or perceive a metaphysical soul in humans. Science has proceeded a further step and has conceived the idea there is no soul, and ignores the notion. Utilizing quantum physics' fundamental principle of super-positioning, other dimensions do exist, and it is possible that the relative forces and energies of the physical human form is only one possible state, and that other possible states or configuration can also exist as a soul to inhabit other dimensions.

Science and Soul

Science is a most useful tool in the effort to observe the unobserved, to make visible what is not visible, and to detect cause and effect change. The question for science is, what began the relative motion of the environment and life? The most prevalent answer to this question in the past and even today, is that an unobserved human-like god is the impetus for all moving things. In contrast, science utilizing observation, measuring, and testing discovered that the change of one thing changes another, and that cause and effect change moves all things into and through relative existence.

Some physicists and cosmologists claim that in an eleventh dimension, membranes collide to change into the explosion of the Big Bang, and the membrane impact fragmented into super strings, that in turn changed into particles, evolved to energy of elements, and eventually to environmental forms, and living forms. Grand imaginative theory but of course what changed to bring the membranes and the eleventh dimension into existence?

There has to be an unformed former of the later relative membrane forms and the dimension in which the membranes exist. There has to be a metaphysical and unmeasurable cosmological force from which dimensions evolve and from which they come into existence.

Soul Dimension

For many people, the writings and teachings of theistic religion are accepted as revealed truth from a human-like god. In reality, the religious statements are mere human dogma.

The word dogma means, "accepted over time as authoritative, not open to question, and regarded as true." The dogmatic statements of theistic religion constitute a failure to recognize the function of the human body to be a metaphysical soul, and the failure to trace life to the environment, and beyond to energy and relative forces, to an impersonal cosmological force.

If a relative function such as a soul exists, then it is possible to perceive and observe it in some way. If human life is related to other life forms, then it is possible to notice a soul function in other life forms. The biological-psychological drives of hunger for food, sex and reproduction, and aggression, are a relative triune force, as a continuation of a cosmological force. All of existence is in motion derived not from a greater intelligence or reason but as a continuation of a single cosmological force.

From viruses, to bacteria, to multicellular life forms, to humans, the innate driving triune soul force of hunger for food, sex and reproduction, and aggression function inside of all life forms. Death brings an end to the physical body but the soul force as a continuation of an indestructible cosmological force, will continue. Once the physical body dies, what has moved it to survive will continue as a coherent force that moves through dimensions of existence.

If something within humans survives physical death, it does not do so passively but in an active way. An active and vital force that contributes to the survival of life also contributes to surviving physical death. The relative triune force of hunger, sex, and aggression that enables life to survive, also extend beyond biological life to survival in an afterlife.

The reality is that all relative motion must be traced not to a human-like god but to a cosmological force containing other dimensions. Death is a "dimensional shift" from earth to another dimension. Reality is not confined to the dimension of earth and what can be observed from such a narrow vantage point. Based on discovery and theory, reality is a continuum that includes other dimensions.

Fear of Death

Fear is defined as "an emotion, a physical or behavioral response to a threat of danger, harm, evil, pain, or to escape a threatening object or situation." Every individual fears injury and so naturally fears ageing and the greater final injury, death of the body. The conscious and subconscious brain/mind wants to avoid the inevitable decline and death of the body. Fear arises when perception occurs of eventual or impending death of the physical body and with it oblivion of mental functions.

Fear of death occurs by focusing conscious attention more on the body with an excluding of focus of attention and comprehension of the triune subconscious force of the human soul. Sensing or imagining the decline and destruction of the body, attention incorrectly sees hunger, sex, and aggression only as functions of physical body organs, the genitals, intestinal tract, and bones and muscles. By so doing, this acquired and shared narrow cultural view fails to perceive that the motion of the body, to be a continuation of an indestructible cosmological force. This being so it is possible for the triune soul force to cohere as a super-positioned pattern in a nonphysical dimensional reality.

Many Dimensions

The word dimension is defined as having a quality of "size, mass, length, time, space, range, or level." Since the process of evolution is a proven reality process occurring within the dimensions of height, width, depth, and time of the earth, there is a probability the process also exists in other dimensions.

There are a range of differing dimensions of existence that life on earth has evolved into through time. Beginning in the dimension of water, life evolved to the dimension of breathing air, then evolved to the dimension of land, and later flying. There are environmental dimensions of mass and size of suns, moons, asteroids, comets, and planets. On the earth exist dimensions of height, width, depth, and time, and dimensions of temperature, air, water, and land. In the present earthly four dimension reality, various animated forms of life exist.

On the dimension of the earth surface exist microorganisms, insects, reptiles, birds, mammals, primates, and the evolved human species. Within the interior dimension of the earth environment live insects, molds, fungi, exquisite tasting French and Italian truffles, worms and animals such as moles live at different levels within the soil. Animals such as beetles, crayfish, crickets, frogs, and fish species, millipedes, mites, mollusks, salamanders, shrimp, spiders, and other animals dwell only in cave environments. Extremophile bacteria have been found to live in the dimension of rock layers nearly two miles beneath the surface.

Animated life exists in the dimension of water. Various fish and mammals such as dolphins and whales live in the five zone levels of the oceans, and fish and mollusks in the many lakes, rivers, and streams. Invertebrates such as starfish, tube worms, and extremophile bacteria live in the deepest dimension of the ocean such as the Mariana Trench nearly thirty-six thousand feet below sea level where the water pressure is eight tons per square inch.

Many animals dwell and make their living in the dimension of air molecules. In the atmosphere and troposphere dimension of up to ten thousand feet altitude, exist viruses, bacteria, fungi and mold spore, and countless bird, bee, butterfly, insect and fly species navigate through the air. In the stratosphere, bacteria have been found to exist at heights of twelve to twenty-four miles altitude.

The science of physics has found a dimension of relative forces of electromagnetism and gravity, and a dimension of energies of elements. There are as yet unverified and untested cosmological theoretical dimensions of super string theory and M theory. The superstring theory of physics says there are nine dimensions and one of time for a total of ten, and M theory says there is an eleventh dimension as well in which membranes impact to cause a Big Bang. To date, the science of physics cannot say what if anything does or does not exist in the dimensions but at least there are modern theories for the existence of other dimensions.

Other Dimensions

Other dimensions of reality have been reported to exist. There is anecdotal and experiential evidence for afterlife dimensions reported from those who have had near-death experiences, (NDE) and from reliably investigated case study reports of childhood reincarnation memories.

Near-death experience is defined as occurring when a person physically dies and is clinically dead for various lengths of time, then revives and recovers to communicate his or her experience. Stages may include:

1. Being out of the physical body
2. Traveling toward a bright light, sometimes through a tunnel
3. Entering a light perceived as a higher self or a god relevant to a cultural group
4. Seeing deceased relatives, friends, and spiritual figures
5. Having a life review of events from birth to the time of death
6. Wanting to or being told to return to the body

Plato records the earliest account of near-death experience in his story, *Myth of Er,* dating from 420 BCE. Raymond Moody (1944-present) stimulated modern interest in near-death experience, and coined the term in his book *Life After Life* published in 1975. Since then, many researchers have investigated thousands of reports and continue to do so as reported to the International Association for Near-Death Studies (IANDS) established in 1981.

Research by the Near-Death Research Foundation has shown that daily in the United States 774 people have a near-death experience. Research has also found that in the United States and other countries, an average of ten percent of the population has had a near-death experience, and in many cases provided details and convincing evidence of afterlife dimensions.

For over forty years the psychiatrist Ian Stevenson (1918-2007) investigated nearly three thousand childhood cases of reincarnation. Chester Carlson (1906-1968) physicist, patent attorney and inventor of the photocopy Xerox machine, was interested in reincarnation.

When Carlson died, he left one million dollars to endow a chair at the University of Virginia, and a further one million dollars given to Dr. Stevenson personally to enable him to continue to research cases of childhood reincarnation.

In his meticulous research, Stevenson found that when young children recall memories of past lives, they usually do so between two and five years of age. Stevenson and his colleagues found childhood reporting of past life memories to be more reliable and often verifiable than were adult reports. In his choice of focus on young children for his research, I am sure Stevenson would have very much agreed with the words of Oliver Wendell Holmes, (1841-1935) "Pretty much all the honest truth-telling there is in the world is done by children."

Afterlife

The earth environment of three dimensions of space as height, width, and depth are natural. The fourth dimension of time as change is natural. Until recently, the natural dimension of energy of quantum particles, atoms and electrons and elements was unseen and unknown. The unseen natural dimensions of radio waves, radar, infrared, ultraviolet waves, and x-rays once unknown, are now known and utilized.

What is referred to as supernatural, is a continuum of the natural. Any dimension beyond as an afterlife is not separate from other known dimensions but has to be a continuation of other dimensions. The dimension of energy is natural, and the dimension of the environment and life is natural.

Therefore, any other dimension can be presumed to be a natural continuation related to all other dimensions of existence. What is called supernatural can only be another natural dimension, perhaps a place of further evolution, and is not a place inhabited by a human-like god. On the edge of comprehension and the unknown is where the concept of a god is built, and for every theist today the work project is reinforced and continued through ritual and tradition.

A god is a human overlay on the unknown that serves to respond to humans during detrimental changing conditions of life and death. Rather than a human-like god, attention should be directed to comprehension of another dimension of reality and continued evolution, not the theological foolishness of reward and punishment.

Praying to an invisible god is in reality the worship of another unseen dimension. Yet, humans can relate with another dimension only by humanizing it, just as the recently modern human species have humanized the earthly dimension by conceiving of a human-like god to protect and assist them. Humans can eventually learn to appreciate the reality of an afterlife dimension without the unnecessary control of it by an imagined human-like god.

The worship of a human-like god is the worship of another dimension as a way to rise above and to escape from the earthly dimension. Dimensions are real while a god is unreal. Gods have to exist in another dimension as there is only sporadic and usually implausible interpreted evidence for them on the earth.

The human mind seeks a continuation of personal existence after physical death. Through experience, dream or vision, individuals continue to report another dimension. Of course some will argue that just as the mind manufactures a human-like god, it also manufactures a dimension of the afterlife. Au contraire, there is actual evidence for the existence of dimensions and none for the existence of a human-like god. A human-like god is a conception that is conflated (to fuse or combine) with an afterlife dimension. To perceive dimensions and the deceased does not equate with a god maker of them. A sui generis god is an unreal theological overlay on real human experience of living and evolving in an earthly dimension of existence.

Reality may also consist of a continuing evolution into the super-nature of an afterlife dimension, a place of continued evolution to higher levels, devolution to lesser levels, or return to the earth. From a single cosmological force comes the impetus of all relative motion of the environment and life, and the reality of differing dimensions.

Analogically speaking, as fish glimpse mammals on the land limited to near the edge of the water, so humans glimpse deceased relatives and friends sensed or seen for brief moments appearing from the dimension of an afterlife. For fish, the land extends much further beyond what can be glimpsed, just as do other dimensions and afterlife dimensions extend beyond limited human vision. Fish have only a vague awareness of the dimensions of land, sky, and air that exists beyond the watery horizon, and those that move about on the dimension of dry land and birds on the wind.

Fish in the dimension of water can only catch brief glimpses of land species that would be considered by any fish as super and beyond fish nature. From a fish point of view, mammals with their ability to move across a distant unknown dimension of land and air, would be regarded by the fish as gods. But they are not gods and exist on another dimension of dry land, an existence the fish can only glimpse. In reality, the mammals are distantly related to and are an evolved species from the dimension of water and fish, now living existence in and on the dimension of land. There are no real gods, only evolving and differing ways of existing in other dimensions.

In the same way as fish live in the water and catch glimpses of land animals, earth-dwelling humans catch glimpses of ghosts and souls that exist in a dimension known as an afterlife. The afterlife is a dimension of continuing evolution in a greater cosmological evolutionary process, admittedly difficult to perceive and comprehend. At the time of physical death there is a transition from a biological reality to a disembodied reality of relative force. Those who say other dimensions are impossible, are doing so while existing in multiple dimensions of height, width, depth, and time. The cognition of the human brain is limited but that does not mean there is a limit to the existence of other dimensions.

Science and Dimensions

Scientists will smile at what they consider to be a naiveté claim of both a transcendental cosmological force and its immanence in living forms. As scientists they will be quite happy to superiorly drone on about measurable phenomena and relative causality.

They will insist that individual life exists once only and personal oblivion is a permanent return to the elements of nature. For individual human life, general science denies any continuing future existence or evolution. Life they state, is a continuing evolution of the environment, which is a continuation of energy and the pure forces of electromagnetism and gravity, all the result of a once only Big Bang. For science there is an evolution from the relative beginning of the universe, ongoing evolution during the present, but no possible future nonphysical individual evolution, none at all.

Science has a fixed notion that only species evolve but not the individuals of the species. Science also has the arbitrary view that the process of evolution is only and completely physical and lacks a metaphysical basis. At least twenty-five percent of the earth's population are atheists and think of life as a progression from nonexistence to conception, to birth, and from a variable lifetime to ageing, and finally to oblivion and nonexistence. Yet the immensity of reality is much greater than what can be perceived, comprehended, and measured by a three pound human brain.

What is at the end of life is not what is said by science to be oblivion, and is not what is said by religion to be a human-like god, who is said also to be at the beginning of existence. At the beginning there was not oblivion or nothing and there were no gods, only a cosmological force that evolved relative forces, energies, environmental and living forms, and dimensions of existence. At the end of life there is no oblivion and no god, only another dimension of existence.

Inferring there is a cosmological force, it must extend through other dimensions other than the human biological existence of three dimensions of space as height, width, and depth, and change of time. After physical death of the human body there may be a transition and continuing evolution.

Death is not oblivion as per science, or entry into the presence of a human-like god as per religion. Humans enter into a dimension of continuing evolution. Some souls may not remain, as based on case study evidence of near-death experience and childhood reincarnation.

There is a tendency for some to devolve, to sink back to a less evolved willing and knowing of earth existence, to repeat the familiar and inevitable struggle and conflict of life.

As regards an afterlife, what are known as gods and goddesses, are metaphors for evolved human souls that exist in an evolved dimension of reality. What is called a god refers only to a dimension humans may have previously visited but have left there to be living now. A present or future existence is not a reward or punishment by a god but a reward or punishment of individual willing and knowing. Human willing is both subconscious and conscious. Why some enter and then leave a more evolved dimension of reality to return to earth is that humans exist mostly in a subconscious and habitual pattern of willing and knowing, as a sequence of cause and effect.

For humans there is death of the physical body but not what human cellular and mental willing are a continuation of, an indestructible cosmological force. Therefore an individual human will go on, and willing and some memory will continue to exist. Living humans store memories in physical cells. Yet, a cosmological force as an immanent continuation that grows human form, may also retain individual patterns of willing as memory and can continue to coherently exist.

The science of physics has demonstrated that quanta and atoms, and electrons move in a circle. From smallest to the largest structures of spiral galaxies observed by astronomers and cosmologists, all moves in circles. Planets and moons move in circles through the solar system. In the night sky one can observe the circular rotation of the earth as the stars and constellations move by as the earth rotates, providing cycles of day and night. Based on research reports of near-death experiences and childhood memories of reincarnation, there is also a circular cycle of life and existence.

Advocating for an afterlife dimension of existence, the question might be asked, for what purpose? The only purpose seems to be to further learn and evolve. Life is a long lesson in willing and knowing, and the afterlife is a place of an evolving progression. Theistic religions point to and promote faith in an afterlife, but do not speak of a process of afterlife evolution.

To evolve and progress through an afterlife dimension of existence, an individual has to train and discipline his or her willing and knowing while on earth. Evolved ethical individuals living on the earth offer a glimpse of the possible quality level of willing and knowing after death.

Religious Dimensions

The theological insistence that there is a human-like god is the falsity of religion. When Jesus spoke of a human-like god as a father, he used the term as a comforting metaphor for a cosmological reality. When he spoke of "many mansions" he spoke realistically. Recognizing that the statement occurs only once in the gospels, and assuming the quote is genuine, Jesus states, "In my Father's house are many mansions: if it were not so, I would have told you." (John 14:2) The truth that Jesus sought to communicate was the truth of human potential and the reality of another dimension adjacent to the struggle of the earthly dimension.

A human-like god is a human artistic word-portrait depiction and a thoroughly false view of religion. The only truth of religion is that reality consists of differing and interconnected dimensions. A human-like god is often accepted as having and dwelling in an after-life dimension. In reality an imagined human-like god is conflated with the reality of another adjacent dimension. The conceived human-like god is false and while a perceived afterlife dimension is true.

The reality of multiple dimensions of existence is most difficult to investigate. Yet, there exists convincing evidence of near-death experience, researched and documented childhood memories of reincarnation, and research conducted with authentic mediums who can convincingly communicate with those in another dimension. In contrast, there is only a blind faith and no evidence at all for the existence of a human-like god.

Place of Rule

A true savior of future humankind will not attempt to destroy evil external enemies, but will instead direct attention to an ascetic effort to reduce expression of the internal triune soul force of hunger for food, sex and reproduction, and aggression.

The Northern Israelite teacher, Jesus, said that the kingdom of the god, or that which rules life, is within. The kingdom is within as three strong ruling forces of hunger for food, sex, and aggression. This triune force is a continuation of a mono cosmological force and is the true trinity. The struggle of the saintly seer Jesus was with an immanent ruler inside himself, but this part of his brief life story was deemphasized in favor of a projected and separate outside human-like god.

The English phrase "kingdom of god" is in Greek, basileia tou theo. The Greek word basileia means, place of a ruler, or a place of rule. The philosopher Plato writing in his work the *Critias,* uses the word basileia to refer to the central building in the ancient city of Atlantis. The later Roman word basilica was a building used by government authorities for public administration. Jesus made use of the phrase "kingdom of god" in the following ways.

"And when he was demanded of the Pharisees, when the kingdom of God should come, he answered them and said, The kingdom of God cometh not with observation: Neither shall they say, Lo here!, lo there! For behold, the kingdom of God is within you." (Luke 17: 20-21)

What Jesus means in this verse is clear as far as where the ruler is located but is not clear as to what the ruling god is. The ruling god within is a word symbol for a cosmological force that rules within as an immanent triune soul that grows the human body to live as hunger for food, sex and reproduction, and aggression.

In the Gnostic gospel of Thomas verse 3 Jesus says, "If those who lead you say, 'See, the kingdom is in the sky,' then the birds of the sky will precede you. If they say to you, 'It is in the sea,' then the fish will precede you. Rather, the kingdom is inside of you, and it is outside of you.

In verse 113, the disciples ask a question of Jesus to which he replies. "When will the kingdom come? "It will not come by waiting for it; they will not say: It comes here, or it comes there; but the kingdom of the father is spread over the earth and yet none see it."

These verses plainly state that the kingdom of the god cannot be observed or seen, is inside of humans, outside of humans, and is spread over the earth. What Jesus speaks of is a relative immanent force in individuals and all things, including the soil of the earth that supports and grows all of life. In another New Testament verse Jesus states: "And he said, So is the kingdom of God, as if a man should cast seed into the ground; And should sleep, and rise night and day, and the seed should spring and grow up, he knoweth not how." (Mark 4: 26-27)

The meaning of the verse is that the unknown inside force that causes seeds to spring up or sprout and to grow, is the kingdom or place of a ruling cosmological force, immanent as that which moves and grows living things. Jesus further said, "Another parable spake he unto them; The kingdom of heaven is like unto leaven, which a woman took, and hid in three measures of meal, till the whole was leavened." (Matthew 13:33)

The verse clearly states there is a vital force but no human-like god or an afterlife dimension within a loaf of bread. An unseen immanent force leavens, expands, enlarges, and grows and obviously nothing human-like or an afterlife dimension exists in the leavening of dough. Jesus also states:

"For the earth bringeth forth fruit of herself; first the blade, then the ear, after that the full corn in the ear. But when the fruit is brought forth, immediately he putteth in the sickle, because the harvest is come. And he said, Where unto shall we liken the kingdom of God? or with what comparison shall we compare it? It is like a grain of mustard seed, which, when it is sown in the earth, is less than all the seeds that be in the earth: But when it is sown, it groweth up, and becometh greater than all herbs, and shooteth out great branches; so that the fowls of the air may lodge under the shadow of it." (Mark 4:28-32)

These words say that the ruler dwelling within is the kingdom but does not contain a king. Within is a ruling immanent force indwelling the earth that brings forth the blade, the ear, and the barley corn. An unseen yet immanent cosmological force in the grain of a mustard seed, grows into a large shrub of up to fifteen feet high.

The kingdom is here at a place and this is what Jesus meant when he said, "And saying, the time is fulfilled, and the kingdom of God is at hand." (Mark 1:15) The kingdom of god is now and touchable by comprehending it. Yet, theological anthropomorphism keeps getting inserted in the way of seeing. The kingdom of god inside a person is not an anthropomorphic presence, just as the outside origin of existence is not a human-like god. A human-like god is only a metaphor to identify an unknown surround of a cosmological force that is also immanent.

Jesus said the kingdom of god is at hand. The English translation of the phrase "is at hand" comes from a Greek word, engiken, meaning, has come near. The Hebrew version of the Greek word is karav, meaning, to be at, or where something is. Using the English phrase "is at hand" or the Greek word meaning, has come near, implies that the god is close by in the future but is not actually present now. In contrast, the Hebrew word karav, means, here or in this place.

The ruling force is present as now time. The ruling force within life is expressed as the force of survival, the generating triune force of hunger for food, sex and reproduction, and the use of aggression. This triune force is a shared immanent relative continuation of a single cosmological force.

As for seeing the ruler within, "Jesus answered and said unto him, Verily, verily, I say unto thee, Except a man be born again, he cannot see the kingdom of God." (John 3:3) The English usage of the phrase "born again" is a translation of the Greek word metanoia, a word consisting of meta, beyond, and noia or noeo, to look. What the phrase means, is to look beyond the surface of living forms. Jesus did not say, will see the place of the ruler in a future sense but said "cannot" now see the kingdom of the god, meaning an immanent force within.

A saying by Jesus from the gospel of Thomas states, "If you do not fast from the world, you will not find the kingdom...." (Verse 27) The daily life of humans is noisy and there are many distractions. The average individual is kept busy with the duties of work and family life, and does not have the time to look beyond the surface of reality and will not find the ruling force within. A dedicated individual who seeks the true ruler of life must fast from the world of temptations and distractions.

Many ignore the evidence for the immanence of a cosmological force and argue that the kingdom of god is only a future afterlife dimension. So says the Catholic Church and in so doing brazenly contradicts the words of Jesus by preferring not to recognize the immanent force within but instead emphasizes that the kingdom of the god will come in the future and will be a place ruled over as a kingdom of love, peace, and justice. For the Christian church, the kingdom of God is emphasized only as the time when Jesus will come again to rule over the earth, and will include a final judgment of the living and the dead.

The righteous will be rewarded and the unrighteous punished and Jesus will also defeat all evil forces and Satan. Until the future coming of Jesus and his kingdom, Christian authority figures will continue to manipulate the population. Individuals will continue to struggle with evil forces as they blindly wait for the second coming of the only one who will save them, rather than finding the ruling soul force inside of themselves.

In Matthew 5:3 Jesus says, "Blessed are the poor in spirit: for theirs is the kingdom of heaven." The Aramaic phrase, Malkuta dishmaya, translates into English as, kingdom of heaven. Some theologians argue the phrases, "kingdom of god" and "kingdom of heaven" are interchangeable and mean the same. Other theologians argue that the phrase was used only in the Gospel of Matthew to avoid offending Jewish readers. However, use of the two phrases became non-distinct over time. The meaning of the two phrases differ. The kingdom of god refers to a cosmological immanence within humans. In contrast, the phrase, kingdom of heaven, refers to the importance emphasized by the writer of Matthew, of transcendent survival of physical death in an afterlife dimension.

Jesus was a human son, and like all humans, at the time of death his soul transitioned to another dimension. Since Jesus is said to be the son of a god, both are now synonymous with a dimension that exists beyond the earthly dimension. Jesus is only human, and a human-like god is only imaginary. It is another natural dimension that is real and important.

A human-like god is a projection for the purpose of knowing an external causal origin of the environment and life. In the Garden of Eden story, the first father of the Old Testament was savage, and the father of Jesus in the New Testament is also. The savage first father in Eden cursed humans with evil while the father of Jesus somehow needed the blood of his son and allowed him to be killed by humans. How ghastly is this? Just as some earthly fathers have poor parenting skills, are absentee or neglectful, and fail to support and protect their children, so the imaginary heavenly father has the same traits.

Only the thoughts and emotions of a flimsy faith in a human-like god insulate humans from chance events of nature such as accident, illness, and aggression. Having the feebly imagined faith of a human-like god brings comfort to many. For without a god, humans would live unprotected from the environment and especially from other humans.

The trinity of Christianity is to be realistically comprehended in the following way. The Holy Spirit is a cosmological force from which the environment and life comes from. The Father is a familiar human symbol to make the unfamiliar and unknown non-human cosmological force known by labeling it. By so doing the unseen origin of existence is identified. The Son is a symbol for the immanence of a sole cosmological force in humans, as the relative triune soul force of hunger for food, sex and reproduction, and the force of aggression, displayed by each individual.

Chapter 11

Perfection exists when whatever is is, and whatever isn't isn't.
Zen Saying

Perfection

The word perfect (Latin per, complete, and facere, to do or make) as an adjective means, "having all essential parts, unblemished, precise and correct, absolute, without fault, excellent and complete, certain or assured." To speak of perfection it is necessary to attribute it to something, yet it is difficult for humans to conceive of something unblemished, absolute, complete, and without fault. However, perfection exists in a way humans usually do not consider.

I define original perfection as that from which all things have come, not a theological human-like god but a non-human-like and unlimited singular cosmological force. The only criteria that can be applied to support the view that this undetected cosmological presence is perfection, is that all comes from it. A primal uncaused aseitical perfection began a sequence of related and relative cause and effect change. Why this occurs is unknown. That it does and continues to do so, is by evidence of what exists.

Humans have expanded the limitations of their senses by developing telescopes and looking into a distant space that appears to be without limits. Just in the twentieth century, it has been calculated that the contents of space, as galaxies, stars, planets, and moons are beyond all counting. The only prime evidence to date for the existence of an unlimited cosmological force, is the immeasurable distances of space and the uncountable number of energy particles, stars, planets, galaxies, and living forms. Only from some unlimited cosmological force have these vast numbers of forms come into existence. Based on the immeasurability of space and uncountable material and living forms, it can be inferred that there is an unlimited cosmological force.

True perfection exists in what is unlimited which is exclusively not noticed or comprehended by humans.

What is limited is relative to an unlimited cosmic perfection. An original perfection, in the best way it can be said, discharges, the limited relative perfection of cause and effect change. Few comprehend both of these existent perfections, the original and what and has come from it as an immanence of relative force. Therefore, the beauty of both and the potential for humans as a continuation of perfection, is obscured for all but a few.

Perfection has never been realistically defined. Attempts have been made by conceiving of a human-like god. Yet this conception truly mars the intuitive perception of an unlimited cosmological force that has discharged all into a cause and effect existence. All of the human-like god and goddess personalities ever portrayed either in story or in sculpted visual form, are generated by human thought, as crude artistic visual or word-portraits of perfection. This is a human way of egocentrically saying that what is human-like is perfection. This handicapped human view ignores the perfect continuation from a cosmological force to relative cause and effect motion that brings all inanimate and living forms into a mysterious related existence.

Perception of any kind of perfection has through brief human history been limited to only the delusion of a human-like god, conceived as distant from the problems of existence, and oftentimes as favoring one culture over another. Gods and governments, and competition, conflict, crime, and war are ego-based consequences of this imperfect way of seeing. A human-like god is formed only and completely in human thought. A god is birthed in human thought, during the straining and struggle of life, to explain where things come from, how events happen, why humans should be good to each other rather than evil, and what happens after physical death.

During early years of life, the newborn has no physical ability to care for him or herself and little knowledge to do so. On the other end of life existence, is old age and a diminished physical ability to care for oneself and less knowledge as memory fades. In the middle of these two extremes of life is a developed ability to work and earn a living, and to have a family and children. During mid-life maturity, humans have a limited and imperfect ability to prevent accidents, injury, illness, conflict and aggression in relationships.

It is in this milieu of surviving existence where a human-like god is conceived of and accepted as a model of perfection and protection. Most of the human population prefers and depends on a god to save them as they realize they do not have the knowledge, strength, or ability to save themselves.

The message of the Old Testament, Genesis chapter 1, is that from the perfection of a human-like god came a perfect creation. But with the more detailed creating of humans in Genesis chapters 2-3, soon came imperfection as separation from the god, and human evil. In chapter 1 of the mythic story, humans are first portrayed as having a "very good" biological perfection, yet later came cognitive and behavioral imperfection of knowing good and evil, and biological imperfection of ageing and death. The meaning of the myth is the condemnation of humans. The separating sin of imperfection consists of the biological necessity of eating the fruits of life, the necessity of having sex and reproduction, and the aggression of killing animals and fellow brother humans.

Another important function of the subjective reason conceived idea of a perfect human-like god, is that it serves as a model for the potential of human perfectibility. The human-like god of western theism is an unseen artistic word portrait of human potential to improve if not to advance toward perfection. The separation of flawed humans from a perfect god in the Garden of Eden story, can also be seen to convey a poignant comprehension. The story is a lament that humans are separate from their own higher potential, and the word portrait of a perfect human-like god is the straining to achieve a difficult if not impossible behavioral improvement and possible perfection.

For theistic humans there has to be a greater ego beyond the limited human ego, beyond the many imperfect human egos concerned mainly with food, sex, and aggression. Humans need an uplifting human origin and it has to be good. To say humans were the fault of the god would detract from the god's perfection, so Semitic humans had to fault themselves with a sin of separation in the Garden of Eden story.

To find a way to relieve the imperfect experience of hunger for food and killing of animals, sex and reproduction, aggression, ageing and death, humans imagined a first father god. Humans uplifted themselves by conceiving of a model perfection as a human-like god. No earthly human was perfect but at least perfection can be conceived and imagined to at least be human-like and helpful.

Humans are related to perfection but not as conceived to be a human-like first father parent figure. In reality, perfection is a singular cosmological force, from which comes a perfect continuation of cause and effect change of inanimate and animate life forms. Original sin was a subjective cognitive process. The early Jews clearly saw the imperfections of daily life, but refused to accept their first parent figure to also be imperfect. Instead they conceived an immature and childish story of a perfect first father, whose created children disobeyed him with unfortunate results. Based on the research of child psychologist Jean Piaget, (1896-1980) this form of story explanation is precisely what cognitively immature children do. With time and tradition the Genesis immature adult story became dogmatically accepted as authoritative.

Christians portray Jesus to be the son of a human-like father god. Jesus is therefore promoted to be a figure of perfection, and his life of healing, love, and forgiveness are seen as ethical perfections. However, his death as a criminal hanging on a Roman cross as a bloody sin offering of redemption, is the grossest distortion of perfection. Therefore, his physical resurrection was required to portray the perfect ability of a human-like god or Jesus to resurrect the dead, and to continue in a heavenly afterlife.

It is arrogant to think or to suggest that anything human-like had or has anything to do with perfection. Real perfection is not a theological human-like god. True perfection is a cosmological force as the origin of everything. Analogically speaking, a father and mother reproduce by giving a part of their body to form a new life. As a greater origin of life, a cosmological force also gives a relative part to immanently form the environment and living forms. Perfection exists as an unlimited cosmological force, and perfection exists in the cause and effect change of how things have come from it.

Life is a cause and effect continuation of a greater reality of the environment and a cosmological force. However, what is biological and cognitive lacks perfection.

Human Fulfillment

Only humans conceive of perfection to be a human-like god. Other species do not bother about perfection or betterment but instead prefer fulfillment. Humans can better fulfill themselves by comprehending a cosmological force, based on the evidence that all things have come from it. Humans can also fulfill themselves by comprehending the unerring perfection of cause and effect sequence and change that moves all things into a better or worse existence. Realizing all relative motion and change is a continuation of cosmological force that extends into the causal perfection of time, is to take responsibility for further individual fulfillment.

Each imperfect individual exists in imperfect conditions and situations, many of these their own doing. Human religion condemns ethical and behavioral imperfections, and governments legally punish the imperfect behaviors of crime. Humans have to rely not on a subjective hypostatized god model, but on the fact that they are a continuation of perfection from cosmological force to cause and effect change of evolution.

From an unlimited cosmological perfection ever comes the limited yet perfect process of cause and effect change. Coming from cosmological and causal perfection, human behavior and thinking can be better improved. Enlightenment is the experience of fully seeing the perfection of a cosmological force as an ability to bring forth all things, and is also seeing the perfection of a changing cause and effect reality. Enlightenment is to also see individual human biological behavior and thoughts as capable of improvement and fulfillment.

A perfect cosmological force shapes the spatial content of the universe. This is done as a continuation and sequence of cause and effect of perfect lawful change and evolution of energies into material and living forms through time.

An unlimited cosmological perfection has brought about the perfection of cause and effect change and the limiting imperfection of all relative nonliving and living forms. As far as is known, at least on the earth, no other species can intuitively perceive cosmological perfection, or perceive cause and effect perfection. Humans have evolved to a stage of self-awareness to comprehend how behaviors and thoughts can be improved on. Evolving human intelligence is progressing toward a pinnacle of general self-awareness and fulfillment. Life consists not only of conscious reason but is directed by a subconscious triune soul force of hunger, sex, and aggression. Recognizing this, human conscious thinking can better function to direct these subconscious forces and behaviors.

Evolved human intelligence as expressed in behavior lacks perfection. For human reality, relative perfection and fulfillment has to be brought about by effort and discipline, by training. Having a potential to be a jewel, a natural diamond is a cause and effect perfect diamond but with effort and attention humans can shape and smooth it by removing parts and flaws to enhance its natural perfection. In the same way, humans have been naturally perfected through cause and effect to exist and survive but humans can also be shaped and flaws removed or accepted, to increase and direct their natural causal perfection to personal fulfillment.

Human self-awareness has the ability to recognize, develop, and to further improve the cause and effect process of growth within. When cause and effect change is acknowledged inside and outside, acceptance occurs and possibility opens to fulfillment. The way to human fulfillment is to enter through the doorway of the possible. The English word possible is from the Latin word possibilis, meaning, "that can be done," and from the word posse, meaning, "be able." A way open on the path to human fulfillment is through recognizing what is possible and to focus on getting desired reality results.

A particular natural quality can be observed to exist within one's own self or in others. Based on reality experience of having at one time experienced, for example the quality of happiness, in one self, or having observed it in others, it can be confidently asserted happiness does exist.

Accepting that happiness is real, based solidly on observing others or having personal experiences of happiness, then possibility exists and opens for happiness to be further developed. If capable of being developed, then happiness can be improved. If capable of being improved, then happiness is capable of reaching a rough perfection and fulfillment. Effort, discipline, and training are required to do so. It may also be a case of removing obstacles that conceal or prevent the improvement of happiness.

While individual limitations exist, what is possible exists for everyone all of the time. As the philosophy of Existentialism insists, each individual is responsible for their existence, and each learns the way of life through instruction, imitation, and trial and error. The individual is shaped not by an imaginary supernatural trinity, but a real natural trinity, of the environment, biology, and individual thoughts and behaviors. The requirement for at least some success has to be a combination of acceptance, and intentional focus of attention and effort to develop, to improve, and to roughly perfect and fulfill. Following the law of cause and effect this is possible as a human birthright.

For the mass population, aside from a few athletes, joggers, and body-builders, there is little time for improvement of the physical body. Most people do not exercise and many eat excess amounts of foods that include sugars, carbohydrates, fats, and animal proteins. Prompted by the near criminal acts of media advertising, many people consume fast foods containing far too much salt, sugar, and fat. A vast number of the population consume foods and water laced with herbicides, fungicides, insecticides, and pesticides, and foods containing hormones, chemicals, and antibiotics.

There is little time in life for cognitive improvement. Mental health like physical health, is often difficult to develop and maintain. With the human species, the brain has evolved to ascendency over the body, so much so that verbal diarrhea is much more prevalent than physical diarrhea. Too many individuals are plagued by worry, toil, guilt, distractions, lying, psychological disorders, addictions, aggression, and attachments. If an individual is unable to resolve these situations, some seek relief from life in suicide, and what they think is the oblivion of death.

Many humans fail at physical and mental hygiene. Strain, stress, struggle, and suffering soon take their toll on the body and thinking. Humans with rarely a rest continually strain both subconsciously and consciously with the challenges of life. Frequent and excessive straining removes the individual outside of the now moment, and the person cannot just accept, be, and proceed from there in a preferred direction.

A dynamic of chronic straining for what isn't, takes the individual out of what is, and away from an appreciation, satisfaction, and improvement of the now moment. Attention can be disciplined and brought to focus on the pre-sent moment, of what is, as a human body and mind of cause and effect change. What exists in the now moment is the accumulation of cause and effect, of environment, biology, and human psychology of subconscious and conscious thoughts. This overall, is perfection.

Meditation

The recognition of human potential for improvement and fulfillment is obscured by toil and distractions, and by the verbal excrement of media entertainment and meaningless digital communication. The dynamic of potential fulfillment is true for many of the earth's population, and yet sadly the evidence of history shows the carnage of a majority affected with imperfect human comprehension.

For humans the discipline of meditation is a way of intervention to improve life. Meditation discipline provides to reduce distractions, to create a calm place from which to comprehend the non-human like perfection from which all comes.

Human conscious thought is not free; it is conditioned by cause and effect of biological subconscious forces of sex, hunger, and aggression, by relationships, and the environment. Meditation can focus attention to glimpse how personal thoughts and behaviors shape the causal perfection of individual existence, and yet the imperfect results of life. Causal perfection has been comprehended by a number of cultures over time including the Greek view of moira or fate, and the Hindu and Buddhist law of karma.

When cognitive time (sensations structured into images of past, present, and future) is stilled through meditative focus of attention, there exists only biological time. Biological time is a continuation of environmental time, of earth and sun. During meditation, time can be intuited to be a continuation of a timeless cosmological force.

Chapter 12

Freedom from worries and surcease from strain are illusions that
always inhabit the distance.
Edwin W. Teale

Strain

In India, some 2500 years ago, a man came to be known as Buddha, the awakened one. He proclaimed a view of existence that life was dukkha, meaning, ill-fit-together, and suffering. The Buddhist Paticcasamupada of dependent causality states that from a place or dynamic not seen, avidya, meaning ignorance, came willing (sankhara) resulting in the body, mind, karma, and an existence of dukkha or parts and thus suffering. Buddhist teachings did not say anything about or attempt to describe what the objective place that was unseen, and from which willing individuals come into existence.

Just about two hundred years ago, a German philosopher by the name of Arthur Schopenhauer (1788-1860) wrote of the "thing-in-itself," the essence of all that exists, that he referred to as "will." He advocated that a cosmic will generates all into an existence of struggle and strife, and that individual human willing is a continuation of this. Schopenhauer spoke of a cosmic Will and an individual will as both the objective and subjective origin of existence. The word will, fits the cosmic dynamic of where things originate from, but is too close to anthropomorphism and the willing acts of human-like gods. His philosophy, like the Buddha before him, is considered to be pessimistic.

Being influenced by both of these Aryan traditions, I would like to add a slight additional insight to these two notable views. As Buddha claimed, existence certainly consists of parts and suffering, and as Schopenhauer claims, there is a cosmic will that brings forth objects and is continued in human willing of the body, and the brain/mind that represents all objects as images. The human will and knowing brain/mind then proceed through a life existence of strife.

Continuing in the tradition of such prominent forebears, and not saying anything radically new, I only add a word, a mere glint on a single small facet, on the greater jewel of their promulgated truths so as to better illuminate the dynamic of existence. I take the word "strain" to be a more descriptive synonym for the words suffering and willing of existence. It can be said that to exist and to live is to willfully strive as per Schopenhauer, and to live is to suffer as per Buddha. Both views imply and suggest but do not specifically mention strain. Strain as effort is a coefficient of will, and strain is a precursor and a precondition which can readily lead to suffering.

The word that most nearly describes and connects both a cosmological beginning and life experience is strain. Whether a Big Bang explosion happened or not, from a singular non-existence sans relative things, there can be inferred some sort of effort and perhaps strain that brought or burst forth relative existence. All living things continue to exhibit a cosmic heritage of strain to exist and to live during this very minute, hour, day, and year.

Life existence consists of strain, straining into existence, straining through existence, and a straining to not go out of, or a strain to go out of existence. While life does consist of parts and suffering, and individual willing consists of frustration and strife, strain is the actual effort and common denominator that occurs and that to which humans can readily relate with experience. Straining to exist or not exist, to have or to avoid, is the dynamic that leads to suffering as noted by Buddhism, and the willing of conflict and strife that engenders the pessimism of Schopenhauer.

Strain is variously defined in the dictionary as "to exceed a limit, to forcibly push or pull, to cause deformation in body or structure." These definitions can be comprehended to be relevant to a cosmological force of all existence that underwent a deformation of its singular form. It exceeded a limit to forcibly impart and so push and move all relative forces and energies of elements and forms into existence.

Further dictionary definitions of the word strain include, "the damage that results from physical or mental exertion, tension, to injure or weaken, overexertion, to strive after an object or goal."

These definitions can be comprehended to apply to the experience of living forms and humans.

A singular cosmological force strains and imparts, to then exist as immanent momentum as relative nonliving, and living forms that by chance or intention, mildly or intensely, strain against and oppose each other. This causal change can be both inferred and observed as effects. Galaxies, stars, suns, planets, moons, and asteroids in a sense, strain and differ through the attraction and repulsion of magnetism and gravity to oppose, and through impact to reduce or destroy each other's existence. All living forms differ with and strain against each other to exist. From a cosmological force and the environment, strain is passed on as the will to live and endure of living forms. A cosmic force in a sense, strains and imparts relative existence, and continues as the strain and tension of living forms. The straining of life consists of hunger for food, a straining desire of attraction for sex and reproduction, and the strained exertion of aggression.

From an unbroken continuation of the straining beginning of innumerable universes, and the straining forces and energies of elements cohering to form the environment of earth, the cosmological natural heritage of humans is to strain through life. The cosmos, nature, and all of life strain into, through and out of existence. From the beginning, all has and will ever continue straining to exist and to live. The human brain/mind fails to detect the cosmological force that brings all relative things into existence, and cannot detect a real beginning or denouement of this seemingly endless and mysterious journey of relative motion. Previously, only the literary story of Genesis existed as an explanation. Even in modern times, the probability is that science will fail to detect an unseen and unmeasurable cosmological force.

Life strains to exist and for as long as life lasts is permeated with light, to moderate, and severe strain. In the reproductive act there is the strain of a sperm to reach and penetrate the egg of the female. There is straining growth and confinement in the mother's womb, the strain of exiting the mother through the birth canal or through Cesarean section to be expelled into the straining of an individual dependent and vulnerable life.

Everyday life is a strain to exist. It is often a strain to awake in the morning, to get to one place and from another, such as work. There is a certain amount of strain to keep a job, to save money and pay bills. Strain exists to get into a relationship and the strain to get out, strain to get along with a spouse, children, relatives, friends, coworkers and fellow humans. There is a strain to nourish oneself and stay healthy, a strain to have the house or car repaired, a strain to make choices in life and to have good results, and a strain to obtain pleasure and avoid pain. Humans strain hour by hour through life, at times comforted with only a strained hope that life will get better sometime in the near future.

Ever dependent on the environment, humans experience the greater force of nature that strains against them and that humans strain against as weather of wind and storm, drought and cold, floods, earthquakes, tornadoes, and hurricanes. The strain of life easily increases to stress, can further increase to suffering, and can increase to violence. There is a straining of hunger for food by the body every few hours. For those who have reached puberty there is a straining tension for sex every few days on average, and associated with this is the straining of emotions, thoughts, and behaviors to love and be loved. There may be straining at any hour of emotions, thoughts, and behaviors of aggression. Humans strain to have certain experiences, such as relationships, money, possessions, and knowledge, with only respites along the way. Each individual strains to obtain and strains to retain.

Life is a strain to exist. The individual strains for him or herself, strains to help others, or strains against others. Even in restful sleep the body is undergoing the quiet strain of cellular repair. Each individual has to reduce the strain of ignorance through learning, and reduce the strain of diet on the body through proper nutrition. Recognizing the truth of the strain of existence, the individual has to best arrange life to reduce strain to a tolerable level. Taking a vacation an individual can rest from strain of work and routine. Not all strain is harmful as the individual can maintain health and fitness through the light to moderate strain of exercise. Intentional strain of exercise sessions develops fitness, health, and strength to better handle the strain of living.

Religion and Strain

The observable and verifiable experience of the strain of evolved life patently contradicts the false story of theistic Middle East religion. The Garden of Eden story imagines a time in a perfect paradise when humans did not strain to exist, a story that is not in keeping with observation which easily sees that the environment and all of life has, does, and will ever strain through existence. In reality, a human-like god story, is the conceived result of the human strain to comprehend where the environment and life came from, how present events occur, and where if anywhere the essence of life may go after physical death. Human-like, is the mid-ground between human and an unknown un-human reality. A human-like god is an artistic word depiction of not knowing and human ignorance, the strain of limitation and lack of comprehension of a cosmological reality.

The conceived theological notion of a human-like god has been accepted by over half of the seven billion population on the earth. Yet popular acceptance is no guarantee of truth. To portray what happened in the relative beginning of the cosmos cannot be sanely accomplished by the use of a human-like god. However, it is safe and sane to say there was some sort of straining as an exertion of force and energy to bring or burst forth all things into existence. A human-like beginning can only be spoken of as an analogy, not as an entity.

There is no evident continuity or relationship of a human-like god with existence or with life, whereas straining has continuity from a cosmological beginning as exertion and effort of force and energy, that continues in the straining of evolving life to exist. Existence came about through cosmological strain and effort of force and energy, not the thought and effortless reciting of words by a human-like god. Straining effort is omnipresent, it exists all around and within, while in contrast there is no evidence of a human-like god anywhere to be found. Gods are only and exclusively found in subjective and egocentric human thought.

The answers that all founders of religion have sought, found, and communicated to others always relate to the strain of life.

On the photo plate of the human mind, a god image was developed to assist in the human strain of existence. A human-like god is a reflex image that occurs as a reaction and response to the strain, struggle, stress, and suffering of human life. A human-like god is a copy of humans, an inward reproduction by human thought, projected outward to the sky beyond, where the attention of the god is then bent and turned back in the direction of humans who accept the blatant hypostatization.

The Middle East religions of Judaism, Christianity, and Islam's answer to the question of life, is that a human-like god created the whole of existence and then inflicted the strain of life as punishment for which humans should be grateful. This aspired to ambivalent optimism is only associated with having of a greater ally in the strain of life, and an ally in the eventual strain of ageing, dying and death. There is no credible evidence that a human-like god expends one iota of effort to reduce human strain in life. Strain and suffering engenders a male god that serves only to give humans a false sense of security and protection so as to be able to carry on in life.

In the Garden of Eden story, the serpent, later said to be Satan, are the counter-symbols of a human-like god to explain the strain and struggle of existence. The first humans were and continue to be blamed for wanting to know more "… ye shall be as gods, knowing good and evil," (Genesis 3:5) and were exiled from a strain-free paradise. Since the imagined event, the imagined human-like god never acts to reduce human straining through life, as all individuals including the ethically good and ethically bad seem to suffer equally.

The human-like god will even impose more strain by punishing some individuals both in the earthly life and in an afterlife dimension of Hell. But yet, theology says that only a human-like god can save humans from the very strain of existence the god makes. This is an unthinking and strained incredulous scenario.

To accept the view of a human-like god who controls all of existence, is to have faith in a role model that dispenses both good and evil as reward and punishment. How else can such a vast amount of evil occurring in everyday life be explained?

Recurring daily events of human strain, stress, struggle, and suffering could not all be satisfactorily explained as punishments of a loving god. Therefore as conceived by Zoroastrianism, Judaism, Christianity, and Islam, a secondary evil entity was variously conceived as Ahriman, Satan, the Devil, or Iblis.

Judaism thinks of the Garden of Eden subtle serpent as an evil inclination (yetzer hara) within humans as a residual stain of sin or separation from the god. Jewish scribes later in the Book of Job conceive of Satan as an adversary angel agent of the human-like god. Jews seek to reduce the strain of social existence by following some of the 613 commandments of the god to have shalom or peace. Judaism says, obey the commandments and social strain will be reduced and the human-like god will not punish the individual or the group, and will parentally punish both if the commandments are not followed and practiced.

Jesus fasted for forty days and nights in the desert and was tempted by a devil, an allegory or symbolic story that represents the strain of earthly life. Jesus strained with hunger for food and was tempted to turn stones into bread. Jesus was offered the role of world ruler but would have had to competitively strain to be the greater aggressor over other aggressive earthly rulers. Interesting is the temptation by the devil, of tempting Jesus to jump down from a high place, to intentionally get the human-like god to respond and save Jesus. The act is a plain danger to the blind belief that a human-like god exists, as an imaginary god will not ever intervene and save any falling or straining human. This is plainly the temptation to violate and question faith and trust in the conceived idea of a human-like god.

The straining for earthly sex by Jesus is not specifically mentioned but is implied as he was alone during the forty days. According to Catholic doctrine and tradition, Jesus was celibate during his life. Jesus sought to reduce social strain upon the earth through teaching love and forgiveness, the individual practice of which can bring peace and rest. "Take my yoke upon you, and learn of me; for I am meek and lowly in heart: and ye shall find rest unto your souls." (Matthew 11:29)

Christianity says the individual should love and forgive one's neighbor and to love and submit to what they share in common, a human-like father god, and then the strain of existence will be reduced.

Love is not a special location in the human body, it is an evolved emotional/mental and hormonal ability. The phrase to "fall in love" means to have affection for someone which is a milder expression of the will to live of sex and reproduction. With love there is also aggression of to "have and to hold" of possessiveness and dominance of a mate, and the mutual consuming of meals of animal and plant forms. There is also a popular saying that, "All is fair in love and war." War is the expression of the soul force of aggression, and since food is required for both of these activities of life, this makes up the triune force of the soul. There is a popular saying that "God is love." Theists like to surround themselves with an imagined greater love as there is very little love among humans. The attribute of love is only borrowed from humans, and in reality human love is a secondary expression of the primary force of sex and reproduction.

When asked which is the greatest of the commandments, Jesus replied that the laws and words of all the prophets are based on two commandments. "Love the lord your God with all your heart and with all your soul and with all your mind. This is the first and greatest commandment. And the second is like it: Love your neighbor as yourself." (Matthew 22:37)

A god is a human word depiction of a cosmological force. A human-like god is a human way of identifying and symbolizing, and organizing thoughts about the beginning, the cause of events, and the ending of life. To love a god is possible only in imagination. In reality, a first father is only a metaphor for a cosmological force from which both the good and the many more evils come into existence. Humans are deceived in life by the theological story of a loving father figure. The love associated with a heavenly father can in reality only be the relief of life by death, and the welcome transition not to the presence of a human-like god but to another dimension.

As an immanent continuation of a non-destructible cosmological force, after death there is a continuation of a soul shift and transition across dimensions.

Love and attraction to neighbors and family members is often problematic, as love is rooted in sex and reproduction. Love is a problem as it is a milder expression of sex and it is also allied with the soul force of aggression that is ever ready to be expressed, and always immediately present or close behind the hunger for food. Attempting to join an individual's irrational soul force of hunger, sex, and aggression, with the irrational soul force of another frequently leads to strain, stress, struggle, and suffering.

The Islamic prophet Muhammad (circa 570-632) retreated from the world to the isolation of a small cave so as to obtain answers to the human strain of social life in his culture. Tradition says he took food and water with him to the cave. Muhammad's revelation experience is said to have occurred during the month of Ramadan, and is today celebrated during the lunar month by fasting from food from sunrise to sunset, and by reciting the words of the Quran. Muhammad was married at the time so he did not reduce his straining for sex, and tradition also says he later had fourteen wives. Since there are one-hundred-sixty-four later verses in the Quran that mention jihad or struggle and aggression, there is little importance of restraining human straining for aggression, especially toward infidels. The importance of Muhammad's revelation was to deliver the message of reducing the straining of life in his society among rich and poor through submission rituals to a greater human-like god.

Muslims practice daily ritual of individual and social submission to a human-like god, and through this method experience salam, or peace in human relationships. Islam says it is okay to strain in jihad against infidels and to strain in polygamy marriages, as long as the individual submits their will five times daily to the human-like god. This theological ploy promotes not straining against the will of the god in any way, and by so doing an overflow effect of not overly straining against fellow faithful worshippers.

Hindus have gods and goddesses to assist them through the straining of life.

The Hindu culture also has something more effective than any popular god, and that is the ancient practice of yoga and meditation. Both direct attention to the immediate observation of the body and mind, and therapeutically reduce the strain of existence occurring therein. The discipline of yoga physical postures stretch and relax muscles, and combined with meditation practice, both reduce physical and mental strain to bring about shanti, meaning peace.

Buddha's answer to the strain of life is not faith in a human-like god, but experiential meditation on the Noble Truths including the Eightfold Path, to enable an individual to reach the ultimate peace of nirvana. Through long days of fasting from food and temptations by an evil story character of Mara who represents the human fear of death, Buddha gained control of straining for food, for sex, and the straining to return aggression for aggression. The result of his efforts was the peace of nirvana.

For both Hindus and Buddhists, those who strain daily on the earth without reaching balance and peace, will continue to strain in the afterlife or reincarnate to earth to strain through a life existence again. A lifetime of straining behaviors, emotions, and thoughts are preserved in the function of energy and memory in the human brain. After death of a physical body and brain of willing and knowing, the energy of which it has consisted, having come from and being embedded in an indestructible cosmological force, remains coherent and continues to strain and so to repeat and recur.

For Hindus and Buddhists there is an afterlife dimension but it is not based on a human-like god or devil. The afterlife dimension is a cause and effect sequence of change, an evolving progression and a situation of "birds of a feather flock together" scenario, of progressing further in the afterlife in good or evil company, or returning to earth and to good or bad company.

There is a straining of earthly life to find peace and relief from the subconscious conflicts within oneself, and conscious conflicts with family members, friends, coworkers, and fellow humans. Individual awareness in a society consists of a dream-like swarm of busy emotions, thoughts, and busy behaviors for food, for sex and reproduction, and swarming of interpersonal conflict and aggression.

For those who strain most in society, the poor and the uneducated and undereducated, the view of a human-like god is most needed and is most accepted. Humans find safety from the strain of life by being a member of a religious group and by sharing the conceived idea of a human-like god. Religious groups seek to be a refuge of optimism in a vast sea of strain on a troubled earth. A human-like god represents the strength that humans do not have, the strength to assist and provide for humans and to reduce the strain of living, dying, and after death.

A popular saying on American gravestones in the past was "Rest in peace," often abbreviated as RIP. The inscription is a recognition that the seemingly endless straining of life has come to an end. The inscription expresses the sentiment and wish that the individual is either at rest until a day of judgment or is in a non-straining place of a heaven afterlife.

A person who attends a theistic religious ritual seeks to be to be in the presence of, to be noticed and heard through prayer, and to obtain a response from, a human-like god. But for the vulnerable individual marooned on earth, the only real higher power is the support and strength of the collective group. Realistically, the conceived model of a god represents the strength of the combined members of the religious group.

Only a greater ego can save the weak and vulnerable individual ego. The conceived ego model of a god serves as a guide through the strain of life on both an unsafe earth and in an unknown afterlife existence. A human-like god is a model to inspire the individual to strain for a higher potential on earth and for a higher potential in an afterlife dimension. Those who accept the view of a human-like god share the multiplied strength of the greater religious group, and via faith this collective strength is believed to continue in the afterlife as elect members of a heaven.

The mass human population continues to comprehend a metaphysical irreality through the vaguely conceived idea of a human-like god. Having a god is to associate with the best.

This is why humans wear nice clothes to a religious service, to look their best, and associate with the best behaviors, emotions, and thoughts in others, and to behave their ethical best. Ethics is then based on this concept of a shared origin conceived as a human-like god exercising judgment of human behaviors. The individual seeks to associate with a human-like god who is the best, has the best intelligence and best strength and power, and who if the individual believes in the existence of the god and asks sincerely in prayer, can remove what is not best and can bring about the best to a fragile straining individual life.

A religious service is a time to reduce worldly strain, a place and time of attention directed to a timeless presence that from the very beginning brought the strain of life into existence. A religious service is a mild strain of attention for an hour, not to comprehend the origin of existence but only to think about that reality from which one's life came from, aside from the biological bodies of parents. A religious service is a rather brief time to direct shallow attention and thinking in an effort to comprehend what the universe comes from and what is good and evil in life. The origin of existence is thought of as a god, rather than the reality of a cosmological force, via its favorite relative direction of circles as atoms and electrons, circular rotating galaxies, and circular cellular functions of life forms.

In the brief allotted time of fleeting surface thoughts focused on the metaphysical mystery of existence, attention may also be directed to better comprehend life on earth among family members and friends. In brief, only if an individual imitates others in theistic religious rituals and has faith, only then can he or she relax individual mental strain to comprehend from what direction and dimension comes the ordering of reality life events. The individual has only to accept the theological prevarication of a human-like god.

Discipline

The word discipline is from two Latin words, disciplina meaning instruction and knowledge, and from discipulus, meaning a disciple, pupil or learner.

Discipline is defined as, "to improve or train by instruction or practice, to produce a pattern of behavior or character, mental improvement, self-control, correction, an area of teaching or knowledge; to enforce obedience or order."

A discipline is to counter outward strain, to enforce, to exert force inwardly. Disciplining and limiting oneself to minimal and moderate straining results in calm and rest, and personal peace. Disciplined lessening of worldly straining brings the individual more and more to a non-straining calm. Fasting is the reducing and lessening of straining for foods. Minimal, moderate, or full celibacy is the reducing and lessening of the straining for sex and reproduction. Pacifism is the reducing and lessening of aggression. Each of these practices of lessening strain can bring individual joy and personal peace.

The obtaining of food brings consumption of it and satisfaction and happiness. So too the opposite, the disciplining and lessening of consuming excess food can bring satisfaction and happiness. Sex can bring the satisfaction and happiness of romance, love, companionship, orgasm and reproduction. Disciplining and lessening the drive for sex can bring satisfaction and happiness of contentment and peace of non-conflict, and peaceful absence of distraction, jealously, and aggression. Expression of aggression can bring satisfaction and happiness of repaying a wrong, retaliation for injury, and revenge. Disciplining and lessening thoughts and behaviors of aggression can bring satisfaction and happiness of safety and peace.

Hindu and Buddhist teachings emphasize the discipline of meditation, calm, poise, exploration of body and mind, wisdom, and forest-dwelling. Only in India does sanity reign with the teachings of the wise minority of the culture. The teachings of India emphasize that both exerting strain for and lessening of strain have cosmological significance. Individual life has a beginning and a journey across a bridge of time, some on the way thinking at the end there is only oblivion; while most think that a human-like god who will either punish or reward, waits on them to arrive.

Only a few wise on the whole earth have the sufficient wisdom to see that their own individual straining constructs the journey of life across a bridge of time. The journey can end by further evolving into another reality dimension, or returning to journey again across the bridge of an earthly existence.

A cosmological force brings forth all of existence and is simultaneously the maker of worlds and immanent in the worlds. Life exists in a surround of an infinite space and time. Individual efforts to survive with behaviors, emotions, and thoughts, predominates to become the hardening habits of an ego, and so a life of an ambivalent love of others by necessity. All things exist as a continuation of a cosmological force. Whoever thinks life existence after physical death suddenly becomes nothing is deluded. As a continuation of an indestructible cosmological force, the individual soul force that has enabled individual biological survival on earth, continues to survive through other dimensions of existence. Disciplining and lessening of excess thoughts, emotions, and behaviors for things brings balance, ineffable peace, and ceasing of continuing existence.

Chapter 13

Happiness is no easy matter; it is very difficult to find it in ourselves and impossible to find it elsewhere. Nicolas Chamfort

Seer

The Christian theologian Saint Augustine (354-430 CE) dogmatically declared that all humans are "massa damnata," a dammed group of concupiscent sinners, separate from a human-like god. The truth is that Saint Augustine has made an error, he made an untruthful and sinful or separating statement. Humans are not separate from that which brings all things into existence. Humans are not a creation of a perfect human-like god, but are a continuation of a cosmological force immanent within them as a triune soul force that is less than perfect, and is not completely good. Humans were not brought into a paradise by a theological god, but were brought into a sequence of time by a timeless cosmological force that evolved as a triune force of survival; as hunger, sex and reproduction, and aggression. Existence is a sin, not as a separation from an outside human-like god but on the inside of the brain as the separating human concept of a god, and the failure to recognize an immanent soul force to be a continuation of a cosmological force.

Existence is also a sin of personal limitations as each person is separate from and is limited to a particular place, family, friends, work, and by time as sequence of change. Each is dependently grounded on the earth and so each is limited. Each seeks to be not limited and this is what a human-like god is utilized for, as a model to remove limitations and to inspire individual potential. Separation is sin, and humans realize they are limited and so separate from an optimum level of ability and intelligence.

A seer is a person who sees. The word seer is defined as, "a person having the ability for extraordinary practical and ethical insight, wisdom, and extrasensory ability." A true seer, sees that a triune force is his lord that moves within.

If the soul force is allowed to go out of control, there is a worldly obsession with food and being severely underweight or overweight. There may develop an obsession with sex and reproduction, with relationships, or if obsessed with aggression, a person becomes a criminal or homicidal.

A true seer seeks to reduce the dark curse within, the strong biological and psychological force of the gnawing pangs of hunger for food, sex and reproduction, and the aggression of thoughts, emotions, and behaviors. The devoted seer seeks to discipline a cosmological force immanent in the body that is reflected in subconscious and conscious awareness. For a seer to reduce, calm, and moderate the devilish triune soul force is to evolve to what religions refer to as a saint, the highest model stand-in for the artistically imagined model of a human-like god.

Most humans, 99.999 percent cannot aspire to be a seer of life. For a seer, the average existence of living for more food, sex, and aggression, becomes a bad dream, and even a nightmare. So as not to imitate the wide way of a generally harmful social life, seers withdraw and separate themselves from the contagious dream-like quality of societal experience, and instead seek quiet seclusion. Seers often utilize ascetic practices by having a minimum of comforts and possessions.

Through meditation discipline, seers reduce the popular practice of cloying for food, for sex and reproduction, and the willing of aggression. Most of life experience consists of one meal after another, repetitive sexual experience, and daily experiences of competition, resentment, conflict, anger, and aggression. These behaviors directed to family members, friends, coworkers, and strangers. For the general population, there is no way out of this willful struggle of existence, only psychotherapy, forgiveness by fellow humans, forgiveness from a god, and death.

Seers clearly see that the function and movement of their own body is a continuation of the mover of the universe. If this is so of oneself, this must be true of all that moves in the universe as forces, energies of elements, environmental forms, and living forms.

When the triune soul force is reduced to a balanced level of function in an individual, that person can deservedly be called a seer.

The primal subconscious forces of the soul cannot easily be ignored or quieted, and can easily overwhelm reasoning activity of the conscious brain/mind. A seer is a person who has succeeded in reducing excess willing for food, sex, and aggression to a seemingly miraculous level of purity and balance. Only a seer knows the way to safety in this world, not a business person, celebrity, politician, general, or a judge.

The seer has recognized that the cosmological force that moves the universe also moves within as the subconscious function of the body that is reflected in conscious emotions, thoughts, and willing of behaviors. A true seer is an individual who comprehends that a theological god exists only as an artistic word-portrait in the human brain/mind, and who comprehends the reality of what the soul is. A seer relies on himself to focus attention and use conscious willing effort to discipline, reduce, and quiet subconscious willing for food, sex, and aggression. Mastery of these main areas of individual willing brings happiness, rapture, and peace.

Christian ascetics imitated Jesus, who in his turn only imitated a much older Hindu and Buddhist practice, that of retreat and fasting from food, fasting from sex and reproduction, and fasting from aggression. The ascetic way of seers is the true encounter with a cosmological force of existence, not an imaginary human-like god but as the three very real soul forces of hunger for food, sex, and aggression, a triune continuation of one cosmological force.

Wisdom is the experiential knowledge that a cosmological force is continued inside living forms. Individual willing is an extension of cosmological force and is therefore difficult to erase from existence. Through gradual unraveling of strands of willing efforts to exist and to have, can the human ego be subdued to relax. Only then can individual willing be perceived as an extension and continuation of an indestructible cosmological force from which the environment and life comes into existence.

Science

A large number of theists credit a human-like god with making life but the god has never evidentially improved life. In contrast, human inventive science has done much to improve the quality of life, through learning, observing, measuring, and testing. Modern science continues to improve life by increasing knowledge that results in better living conditions, such as medicine, nutrition, mental health, housing and transportation. Science also improves the quality of the earth environment, to travel to and exist in the environment of space, on the moon, the planet Mars, and beyond the solar system. Science works to know more and to contribute to a better life existence, and business further develops and markets labor saving technology products to improve the quality of life experience.

Yet as science limps along through life using trial and error learning, as frequently as it improves life experience, science also frequently degrades and diminishes the quality of life. Science contributes to the worsening of the quality of life through chemical pollution of the water, air, and soil, the use of toxic pesticides, insecticides and herbicides on produce, carcinogenic chemical food additives, toxic chemical and oil spills, and global warming.

In reducing contagious illness through antibiotic use, science is increasingly causing the proliferation of antibiotic-resistant super viruses and bacteria. Working to reduce war, science has developed even more frightening weapons of warfare and mass destruction including nuclear, biological, and chemical capabilities. The deficits and excesses of evils abound while the good of balance continues to be lacking.

Can seers better improve the quality of life, or can scientists better improve life? Both are essential to human-kind. Children should be educated in science, and in comprehending the immanence of a cosmological force inside of humans and living forms. Children should be educated not by studying a theological artistic word portrait of a human-like god but in the science of a cosmological origin. Children should be taught meditative exploration of the conscious self and the subconscious soul.

Children should be taught to be seers, and to trace the continuation of a cosmic force to be immanent as the innate will to live of the triune soul force. Acknowledging a cosmological origin of all existence can result in an improved ethics and inventiveness rather than a current dominant profit motive.

A majority of scientists accept the reality of a cosmological, not a theological universe. Based on a 2009 survey by the Pew Research Center in the United States, eighty-three percent of the general population holds the view of a human-like god while only thirty-three percent of scientists do. Science is wary of the use of anthropomorphism and the presence of any human-like god, yet even scientists are not immune from referring to a human-like god.

The physicist Leon Lederman's 1993 book title partially used the phrase, *God Particle* which the media continues to make use of in print and reporting. The combining of the word god with a subatomic particle of the Higgs boson that theoretically enables mass to form, at least suggests a human-like god. In so doing, Lederman and the media both sin against the more sane standards of astrophysics that prefers only the study of forces, energy particles, fields, and grounds.

The challenge of recently modernized humans is to acknowledge the reality of a cosmological heritage and to discontinue use of a delusional theological heritage. Replacing theological saints, cosmological seers can direct attention to learning and to comprehending a cosmological force as a continuation of that which moves within humans and all living things. As of the twenty-first century, theological saints have been too subjective, while scientists have been too objective. In the future, cosmological seers are needed to lead the way for humankind.

Science is the key to improving the quality of life to a balanced, peaceful, and ethical level. The inventiveness of science can provide leisure time, and having this luxury, meditative seers can then sort through subjective emotions, thoughts, and behaviors to refine their cognitive clarity and ethical purity. Life should be lived to cultivate meditation and clarity of perception, to maintain physical health by exercise, and eating quality organic foods.

Individuals need to at least be moderate or minimal in the areas of hunger, sex, and aggression. Gradually through much trial and error learning, patience, and age of years, joy is sure to dawn in the lives of cosmological oriented seers.

Only a minority of any population ever succeeds in obtaining knowledge. Of those that manage to obtain knowledge, only a very few acquire wisdom. The seer seeks to find that which is of true value. The seer acquires wisdom, the ability of how best to use knowledge, acquired through study, association with the wise whether living or not living, and meditation.

Seers meditate, for only through meditation can an individual develop wisdom. In seeking knowledge he finds extrasensory abilities of clairvoyance, telepathy, precognition, and healing. He earns the trust and love of those living that come to him for advice and healing. He finds and correctly comprehends that a cosmological force moves all things into existence and is immanent within him, and he accepts that this force is equally present within all things. In this way he reaches true wisdom and peace. Voila! Metaphysics and ethics merge into one coherent view and practice.

With honesty the seer confronts the interior forces of his existence, sees that his very own relative personal forces are an invisible link with a greater cosmological force of all existence. The seer moderately disciplines his internal relative soul forces, respecting them as expressions of a greater cosmological force of all universes and dimensions. The truth-bound seer by-passes all false theological separating thought of a human-like god, and accepts his calmed relative individual soul force to be a continuation of a greater cosmological force.

A seer comprehends that religion does not observe a human-like god, and that a theist has to rely on faith (Latin fides, trust). He comprehends that cosmology also does not observe a cosmological force, and that it has to rely on inference. However, inference of a cosmological force is based on observation of the relative motion of the environment and living forms. Unlike religious faith, inference is grounded on observation of a continuation of relative motion.

All comes from and is connected to an indestructible cosmological force as a vital animating triune cohering force that clothes its cosmic presence with a shell of energy and form, and without it the physical body functions not and moves not at all.

The seer may meditate by focusing attention on an area of the body, to examine and bring to an end all strain, in and among the parts of the body. In place of stress and non-awareness, rest and bliss arises among the parts for seconds or minutes. Both internal straining, and straining with what is external, at least temporarily ceases. Straining among internal body parts and straining of emotions and thoughts with what is external comes to an end. Rest and bliss arrives when strain departs; where there is no straining of body and brain, rest and relaxation arises. When strain ceases and when rest and bliss pervade body and mind, clarity of perception arises and continues. This clarity will fade without meditation practice.

The average person thinks of what they are as the conscious aware self, the biological body, and the individual sees the functions of sex, hunger, and aggression, as only physical. What a person is, is what has grown them and enabled them to better survive; a subconscious organizing soul force at the basic level of cellular function and the autonomic nervous system. The organizing soul forces of sex, hunger, and aggression are a continuation of organizing relative forces, energy of elements, the environment, and all a continuation of a sole organizing cosmological force.

The seer sees hunger for food, sex, and aggression, to be a soul force and a continuation of a cosmological force. Soul as an organizing triune force has a dual role, the one for physical survival, and the other as a force also capable of surviving death of the body. The soul force can survive physical existence as it is rooted in a single indestructible cosmological force of all that exists. The relative functioning triune force is the metaphysical soul, that which survives physical existence. A cosmological force pervades all, and does not exclude but includes dimensional properties.

As the experimental method did not exist until recently, there exist countless anecdotal reports through history of the deceased as spirits and ghosts appearing, heard and felt from another dimension.

While not experimental evidence, the sheer number of these anecdotal reports over many centuries supports the view of other existent dimensions.

A cosmological force immanent in all is indestructible, and cannot be destroyed, only the inanimate and animate gross form is destroyed. To see this is wisdom. Eventually, all life forms lose the contest of life through inevitable accident, aggression, illness, and ageing but will not be totally lost to oblivion. An unseen continuity of an indestructible cosmological force ever links both nonexistence and existence, and dimensions.

Denouement

The soul force of hunger, sex, and aggression is natural, and nature has been discovered to be a connected flow of energy elements and relative forces that compose environmental and living forms, that in turn all flow from a cosmological force. The discovery of this flow of energy and the repeated confirmation and utilization of it is a scientific testament of truth. This objective testament of science sanely replaces any and all subjective testaments of a human-like god.

Through time humans will eventually develop the comprehension that a human-like god is only a human way to speak of a cosmological force that shapes all that exists. In time the dim light of evolving human comprehension will lift the veil of the dark shade of ignorance to reveal a cosmological origin. Then no longer will praises for a human-like god be heard to echo on the earth, and no longer will plaintiff prayers be heard for a soul to be saved.

When superstitious thoughts and behaviors of religion are replaced by reaching full cognitive maturity, then will be heard from some sizeable portion of the population, a dirge, a tearful recognition and yet true lament that life is on its own on planet earth. Those who reach individual cognitive maturity, will realize that all references to a human-like god only compose an artistic word portrait that represents higher human potential and protection.

Further lament and weeping will also be heard when the soul is perceived to be the root cause of problems for evolving human intelligence. It will be realized that the soul does not need to be saved by a god as it is a continuation of an indestructible cosmological force, and is by default saved by cause and effect.

With the assistance of seers and scientists as role models, humans can survive the environment, microorganisms, and the greater threat of each other. Failing this, the human population will continue to live an overcrowded scrambling lifestyle similar to rats and roaches. There must develop a way of recognizing each other not only as family and friends, but on the experiential and ethical basis of seer and scientist clarity.

To accomplish this Herculean feat, a human-like god will have to be comprehended for what it is, a strictly human and only partially effective way of reaching toward a higher human potential using a utilitarian artistic word portrait. The human soul will have to be recognized for what it is, an immanent force as a continuation of cosmological force.

The soul force of hunger, sex, and aggression, will also have to be comprehended as not only enabling survival of an earthly dimension of existence but is also capable of surviving in other dimensions. If egocentric differences can be put aside to accept similarity and cosmological kinship, maybe and only then, will there be a future chance for mutual respect and love to finally dwell amongst members of the human species.

www.ingramcontent.com/pod-product-compliance
Lightning Source LLC
Chambersburg PA
CBHW071350280326
41927CB00040B/2574